S0-BEF-651

THE
GERMAN ELEMENT
IN THE
OHIO VALLEY:
Ohio, Kentucky & Indiana

By Gustav Koerner

Translated and edited by
Don Heinrich Tolzmann

CLEARFIELD

German-language edition
originally published
Cincinnati, 1880

Translation by Don Heinrich Tolzmann
Copyright © 2011
All Rights Reserved

Printed for Clearfield Company by
Genealogical Publishing Company
Baltimore, Maryland
2011

ISBN 978-0-8063-5507-8

Made in the United States of America

CONTENTS

Editor's Preface

In 1880, Gustav Koerner (1809-96), former Lieutenant-Governor of Illinois and confidant of Abraham Lincoln, published a comprehensive history of the German element in America: *Das deutsche Element in den Vereinigten Staaten von Nordamerika, 1818-48*. (1) Although his focus is on the first half of the nineteenth century, Koerner often goes well beyond that date up to the time his history was published. Going state by state, Koerner provides an in-depth portrait of the German element throughout the country. In the past, I have edited chapters from Koerner's history that focus on the German element in various states, and the present volume is a continuation of that series. (2) For this volume I have drawn together my translations of those chapters dealing with Germans in Ohio, Kentucky and Indiana. Together they illuminate the history of the German element in the Ohio Valley, and how deeply it has influenced the social, cultural, and economic, and political life of the region. For those not familiar with Gustav Koerner I have included essentially the same introduction that I prepared for my translated edition of Koerner's *The German Element in the North East: Pennsylvania, New York, New Jersey and New England*. (Baltimore, Maryland: Clearfield Company, 2010). This provides biographical information about Koerner and explains his basic goals and objectives in the field of German-American history.

Don Heinrich Tolzmann
Cincinnati, Ohio

Editor's Introduction

The Author: Gustav Koerner

Gustav Koerner (1809-96) was a *Dreissiger*, or Thirtyer, as members of the generation of German immigrants were called, who participated in the 1832/33 Revolution. (1) Born in Frankfurt am Main, he had studied at the University of Jena, where he became a member of the German student organization known as the *Burschenschaft*, which had branches across the German states. (2) The *Burschenschaftler* had visions of a united Germany under a republican form of government. After completing doctoral studies at the universities of Munich and Heidelberg, Koerner returned home to Frankfurt am Main, where he became involved in the uprising in 1833, causing him to flee to France. (3) Departing from LeHavre, he sailed to the U.S. and landed in New York, but moved on to St. Louis due to the glowing report of Missouri that had recently been published by Gottfried Duden. (4)

Disappointed with the fact that slavery existed in Missouri, Koerner moved across the Mississippi River to southern Illinois to the settlement of Belleville. This was widely known as the "Latin Settlement," as so many other well educated *Dreissiger* had settled there. (5) It was said that some of the farmers in the area read Latin classical texts while plowing the fields, and some poked fun of them as being more skilled at reading Latin than farming. Nevertheless, the Latin Settlement became a veritable German-American social, cultural, and political center that exerted its influence in Illinois, as well as in nearby Missouri. Koerner comments in his Foreword:

> After the author arrived in America in the summer of 1833, he selected Illinois as his place of residence and decided to practice law, which he had studied for four years at various universities in Germany, and which he had also practiced in his home town, Frankfurt am Main. After studying English, of which he already had some rudimentary knowledge, the next item on his agenda was studying the U.S. Constitution and commentaries about it, and then civil law, especially that of the

state of Illinois. By the age of twenty-three, he completed his studies of American law and commenced the practice of law in Illinois in summer 1835. (6)

Not surprisingly, Koerner quickly got involved in political affairs, and was elected to the Illinois state legislature in 1842, and in 1845 was appointed by the governor to a position on the appellate court and was confirmed in that position by the legislature in 1846. In 1852, he was elected lieutenant governor and was viewed as the leading German-American politician of the state. After joining the fledgling Republican Party, he campaigned for Lincoln, who visited with Koerner at his home in Belleville. (7) As a result of his support of Lincoln at the Republican convention in Chicago and the following campaign, Koerner was appointed U.S. Ambassador to Spain. In the 1870s, he withdrew from active involvement in public affairs, and devoted himself to writing, completing his history of the German element, as well as a two volume autobiography. (8)

Julius Goebel, editor of *Deutsch-Amerikanische Geschichtsblätter* described Koerner's work as a "valuable historical study" and the author as "a keen observer of men, a profound and sympathetic student of American institutions, politics, and life in general, and a man of calm judgment..." He felt that Koerner was "exceptionally well qualified to write the history of one of the great constituent parts of the composite American population during a period the great part of which he had followed as an eyewitness." (9)

The Book

In a lengthy Foreword and Introduction to his German-American history Koerner explains the goals and objectives of his German-American history, which can be summarized as follows. (10) He makes it quite clear that his work definitely is not a history of immigration, as he begins not in Europe, but in America and focuses on the Germans in America. He writes:

The author of the present work does not plan on writing a general history of German immigration. This would be adverse to his way of thinking, and be of no interest to him. I certainly make reference to immigration, but only as the foundation for a history of the German element in the U.S. The purpose of my work is to show if and to what extent the German element has influenced American society. (11)

He follows up by emphasizing: "I must reiterate that this is not a history of German immigration, but rather a history of the German element in the U.S., and one that focuses on a particular time period in the nineteenth century." (12) Koerner, therefore, is not interesting in telling the story of German immigration and exploring its root causes in Europe, but rather wants to concentrate on the German element in the U.S. and explore how it has influenced American society.

Another point he wants to emphasize is that he describes the component parts of the population as "elements" and that his particular focus is on the German element, a term that he uses to refer to German-speaking immigrants and their offspring. He notes in this regard:

The nations of the civilized world are few that do not consist of a mix of various peoples, some closely related, but also others that are not. These components of the population are frequently referred to as "elements." It has always been an interesting task to investigate the different influences these various elements have exerted on the life of a given nation, so as to ascertain and measure the extent of these influences. For those of us who live in America such a study has not only academic, but great practical implications as well. (13)

Here he makes it clear why he has written a history of the German element in the U.S. He obviously views the history of immigration as valuable, but that a history of the German element in America would not only be something of academic interest, but would also be of useful to demonstrate how the German element had influenced American society.

x

Having experienced the anti-immigrant Know-Nothing Movement of the 1840s/50s, Koerner no doubt felt that German-American history would assist German-Americans as a means to demonstrate their significance for American society. He writes:

> A clear and correct picture of the role played by the German element in American society and the influence it has exerted and the ways it has been influenced by American society can only be advantageous for us. As this picture becomes clear, it will evidently form the foundation for an ongoing modus operandi of the German element in American society, and it is important that we do not deceive ourselves in being aware of this crucial fact. (14)

In this regard, it should be noted that Koerner states that his aim "is to do justice to the history of the German element." However, and this goes back to his legal training and background, he wants to do so in a judicious manner, stating the facts and not overemphasizing or overly praising the influences that he documents and records. He, therefore, distinguishes his history from a history of Germans in America by Franz von Löher. Koerner critiques him as follows: "While on the one hand he is unjustly critical of Germans in America, on the other hand he overly praises them at times for contributions, some of which are either not theirs, or might not have been as great as he maintains." (15)

The two major points Koerner, therefore, wants to emphasize at the outset is, first, that his work is not a history of German immigration, but a history of the German element, and, second, that his aim is to explore the influence it has exerted in an objective and judicious manner.

Additionally, he has several other related points that he would like to emphasize. Most importantly, he would like to explain his views on the role of the German element in American society, and he does so in response to the question that was widely discussed in the 1830s40s as to whether a German state might be founded on the American frontier. Koerner makes it clear that he is adamantly opposed to such proposals, and that this would be adverse not only to Germans, but to Americans as well, and contribute to the anti-immigrant Know-Nothing Movement of the time. However, it should also be noted that Koerner himself was from the well-known German-American Latin Settlement in Belleville, Illinois and that throughout his work he does praise German settlements as they reflected the reality of German immigration history. He therefore supports the various kinds of German settlements, be they secular, religious, or communitarian, but opposes the notion of a German state as problematic. By means of his own example he demonstrated that members of German settlements could take an active part in American society, but stresses that the notion of a German state would be a move in the wrong direction that would isolate and separate the German element from the mainstream of American life. Here he indicates his agreement with Kapp, who wrote that:

Therefore the goal of the German immigration lays not in separating itself off from the formative elements of the population, nor in fantastic dreams of forming a German state or utopia. It cannot prosper and thrive anywhere off track from mainstream America, but rather by working together with one's fellow citizens can obtain all the success and blessings that are possible here. A German nation within the American nation is impossible, but the richness of German life and the treasures of its cultural heritage can certainly be added onto the scale in terms of its contributions to America. Moreover, the German element's influence can only increase, and create for itself a greater degree of involvement in American life the less it presents itself as separatist. At the same time, it can hold on to all that is great and good that Germany has given to the world. (16)

Moreover, Koerner believes that the German cultural heritage can be preserved, and that it would be unnatural if it was not. Just as he opposes the extreme position of those advocating a German state on the American frontier, so too does he speak out in his history against advocates of total assimilation, who would deny their ethnic identity and heritage. He writes in this regard:

The love of German language and literature should of course be held sacred and transmitted to one's offspring. And, of course, the cherished German cultural heritage that we bear within us can never be lost. That would be ungrateful and foolish, since by preserving and defending this heritage, while at the same time declaring our loyalty to the land of our choice, we honor ourselves in the best way possible, as well as the people we are descended from and for whom our hearts beat with a never-ending love. (17)

This latter point relates to his views on Germany, which he separates from his love of the German cultural heritage. Here he praises the political freedoms of the U.S., noting that: "Once one has been here on freedom's ground with the American people, one will not wish to return to the old Fatherland, but will find one's own place as best one can, unfettered by memories of the past." (18)

His relation to German heritage therefore is cultural, relating to the ancestral homeland and to the background of Germans in America, rather than a political dimension relating to the new German Empire, which as a *Dreissiger* he still takes exception too, as did some of the Forty-Eighters. This is an important point to make, separating his German heritage off from any political associations to the Old Country, and making it an essential cultural component of his own identity, as well as that of Germans in America.

Contextually, Koerner does view the history of early nineteenth century immigrants as another chapter in the history of Germans in America, and as part of this ongoing continuum. In stressing this sense of continuity of German-American history, he seems to be saying that the more recent German immigration not only complements the early German immigration, but also builds on the foundations it had laid. (19)

Although Koerner places his work within the framework of German-American history, he is most interested in concentrating on the German element of the early nineteenth century, especially those who came to America before 1848. A sub-text of his work is that like many of the *Dreissiger*, he felt that the contributions of his generation had been in a sense overshadowed by the more colorful, flamboyant, and vociferous Forty-Eighters. He diplomatically expresses this as follows:

> There are several reasons for closing this work off with the year 1848. To go further would have been a difficult and ambitious task. However, a major reason is that since the 1848 Revolution many individuals with writing abilities have found refuge in America, and there is absolutely no dearth of talent among them for those who want to take on the task of writing the history for the following years. (20)

He therefore assigns the task of writing German-American history after 1848 to another generation, while he takes on the task of telling the story of that of his own. Although Koerner focuses on immigrants who came before 1848, he does follow them and their life up to the period when his book was published in the 1880s, so that his history actually does not conclude with 1848, he is just indicating that his focus is on immigrants who came before that date. His history, therefore, is basically one that concentrates on his generation.

Finally, reference should be made to his approach to writing German-American history, which might best be described as "history as biography." He does not take a topical or chronological, but rather a biographical approach, focusing on individuals as his point of departure of discussing German influences. Here he notes that:

> Although the following is not a history of German immigration and settlement, but rather a contribution to the history of German influence on America, it is not merely a chronological compilation of information relating to this topic. Rather it aims to present a series of biographies of those Germans, who in some way made contributions in this regard. These life histories at times naturally surpass the timeframe of the three decades covered here, especially as this relates to their previous life in Europe. However, I believe that this manner of presenting history will interest the reader, and will attain the goal I have in mind. (21)

The disadvantage of this approach is that he does not cover, nor address all possible topics that might be covered, but the positive aspect of it is that he provides in-depth biographical information on those individuals, who succeeded in adding a German dimension to American life in their particular field of endeavor.

The chapters that follow in translation are those dealing with Ohio, Kentucky, and Indiana, and are drawn from Koerner's German-American history. (22) The original bibliography of primary and secondary source materials in Koerner's history is included for those interested in further reading. Additionally, references to other sources have been provided by the editor in the footnotes.

Chapter One

Ohio, Part I

Ohio – Joseph M. Bäumler's Community in Tuscarawas County – the early German
element in Cincinnati – Martin Baum – Christian Burkhalter – Albert Stein –
Churches – Bishop Friedrich Reese – the Wahrheitsfreund – the Christliche
Apologete – Wilhelm Nast – Political Newspapers – Heinrich Rödter – Character of
the German Press in the 1830s/40s – the German Society – Karl Gustav Rűmelin –
Emil Klauprecht – the German Chronicle of the Ohio Valley – Heinrich von Martels
– Dr. Joseph H. Pulte – Heinrich A. Rattermann

Ohio justifiably exerted a great deal of influence in the early nineteenth century as
German immigration began anew. Just as a group of separatists had been attracted to
Pennsylvania in the first decade of the century, so too did a similar group of
Wűrtembergers come to Ohio in 1817. It blossomed under the circumspect
organizational leadership of Joseph Michael Bäumler, a teacher. The community was
originally not communistic, but necessity drove it to organize itself communally for
business and financial reasons. After overcoming the greatest difficulties, it succeeded in
establishing its new home in Tuscarawas County by means of indefatigable diligence and
heroic perseverance. (1)

Bäumler served as leader of the community until his death in 1853. Although
preaching was open to anyone, Bäumler was the real prophet, serving as judge and doctor
as well. At the time of his death, the community possessed 5,900 acres of land, splendid
cattle herds and mills of all kinds, a cloth factory, carried on a significant trade, and
accumulated a wealth of capita, as well as an unlimited amount of credit.

The village of Zoar, after which its inhabitants became known as Zoarites,
numbers today about six hundred people, and creates the impression of a German village

due to its romantic location and the predominantly red tile roofs of its buildings. Although its inhabitants, with few exceptions, are all born there, German is spoken almost exclusively in the village of Zoar. (2)

In Cincinnati, the real business center of the Ohio Valley, the influence of the German element made itself known early on. Already in the first years of its legal existence as a city (1802) two Germans were elected to the highest municipal office: David Ziegler from Heidelberg (1802 and 1803) and Martin Baum from Hagenau in the Alsace (1807 and 1812). Ziegler was the first mayor of this inconspicuous town. (3)

However, it was particularly Baum (born in Hagenau 15 July 1761, died in Cincinnati 14 December 1831), who in many ways contributed greatly to the tremendous growth and development of the German element in Cincinnati and the Ohio Valley. By means of his great wealth, which he had acquired in various branches of business and which he re-invested, he contributed immensely to elevating the status of the entire West as well. As early as 1803 it was mainly Baum who contributed to founding the first bank of the West, the Miami Exporting Company, whose president he remained for many years. Through this business, which was also a large transportation company, Baum became the most important promoter and developer of traffic on all the western rivers. He founded the first sugar refinery, the first iron foundry, the first wool factory, the first steam flour mill, and other industrial establishments of this kind in Cincinnati. He gave work to numerous people in his various business enterprises, and as he could not find good and skilled workers in the backwoods in sufficient number, he therefore hired recently arrived immigrants in Baltimore and Philadelphia, and thereby directed the stream of immigration to the West. Even the first landscaped garden as well as the first vineyard in the state of Ohio, which Baum laid out at Deer Creek, now in the present city of Cincinnati, herald him as one of the most industrious men of the West.

But it was not only business life that Baum contributed to more than anyone else, as it was also his appreciation of art, science and literature that attracted so many well educated individuals, who then chose to live in the settlement so richly blessed with the beauties of nature. The founding of the Lancaster School (1813) and the Cincinnati College that came out of it (1818) was, next to that of Judge Burnett, mainly the work of Baum. He was also a member of the board of trustees for many years and the first vice-president of the college. Baum was also one of the promoters and co-founders of the first public library in the West (February 1802); of the Western Museum (1817); the Literary Society (1818); the Society for the Improvement of Agriculture in the West (1819); and the Apollonian Society (1823). In 1812, he was suggested as a candidate for Congress, but declined as he did not have the necessary time to be absent from his diverse business enterprises.

When we consider that he was at that time the wealthiest and most respected man in Cincinnati – he was at that time the president of the Cincinnati branch of the U.S. National Bank – that he was in touch with the most important people of the country, then it becomes quite clear that Baum had become a powerful pillar of the German element in its earliest stage of development. At his home, which at that time was the most elegant in the city, he often hosted the great minds of the area, and German scholars and writers were particularly welcome as guests at his home. In 1817, the gifted author Julius Ferdinand von Salis, a cousin of the German lyric poet County Johann Gaudenz von Salis, came to stay with him. According to Klauprecht, he had traveled through the Orient as a naturalist and here in this remote market center of the west was writing his experiences and impressions about the cradle of civilization for a German publisher when death snatched the pen from his hand in 1819. (4)

At the same time, the previous secretary of Prince Blücher, Christian Burkhalter, lived as a recluse at Baum's estate in the Deer Creek Valley. He was born in Neu-Wied, and had immigrated to America in 1816, driven by religious enthusiasm. Later on, he joined the Shakers, who had established Union Village in Warren County, Ohio (1820), where he was visited by the Duke of Weimar in 1826. However, Burkhalter left the Shakers and founded a Whig newspaper in Cincinnati, *Der Westliche Merkur*, which he published and edited till 1841. In this year, the name of the paper was changed to *Der Deutsche im Westen*, published by Burkhalter and Höfle. However, as its success did not

correspond to the efforts put into it, it passed on in the following year into the hands of
Rudolph von Maltiz, receiving a new name as the *Ohio Volksfreund*. Burkhalter retired
from active involvement with the German press, and joined the *Cincinnati Chronicle*,
published by Pugh, Hefley – as Höfle had anglicized his name – and Hubbell, as a silent
partner. In 1836, Burkhalter joined the well-known abolitionist James G. Birney on the
editorial board of the *Philanthropist*, the first abolitionist paper of the country, after the
printing press of Achilles Pugh, the publisher of the paper, had been burned by a mob in
Cincinnati. (5)

In 1817, Albert von Stein arrived in Cincinnati, and acquired an important name
as an accomplished engineer in the U.S. He was the promoter and builder of the
Cincinnati municipal waterworks, which were the first in the country to be driven by
pumps. Later on, Stein drew for Wilson's illustrated ornithology (1823), and since that
time was active constructing water works in Richmond and Lynchburg, Virginia; the
Appomattox canal at Petersburg, Virginia; as well as the water works of New Orleans,
Nashville, and Mobile. Stein was the owner of the latter water works till his death at the
age of eighty-four in 1876, and his family is still in possession of the same. (6)

At about the same time (1817) and shortly thereafter, several Catholic and
Protestant congregations were formed not only in Cincinnati, but also at other places in
Ohio. (7) Dr. Friedrich Reese, a learned, influential, and generally well-loved man, was
the first German priest in Cincinnati (1825), who later became the Bishop of Detroit. He
was born in 1791 at Vianenburg near Hildesheim, and first served in the cavalry before
studying theology. He died in Hildesheim on 27 December 1871 after he was called to
Rome in 1841, having renounced his episcopate. In Cincinnati Reese founded the learned
school known as the Athenaeum, which later passed into the hands of the Jesuits, who
transformed it into the well known St. Xavier College. During his visit in Germany
(1828-29), Reese caused the still existing Leopold Foundation to be formed in Vienna for
the purpose of supporting Catholic missions in need of support. Reese published a book,
Geschichte des Bisthums Cincinnati, which appeared in 1829 in Vienna, and was
moreover also active as a writer. (8)

The following gentlemen were the first German Protestant preachers in Cincinnati: Joseph Zäslein, Jakob Gülich, and Ludwig Heinrich Meyer. It is beyond the purpose of our work to follow the further growth and development of religious denominations here. However, suffice it to say that German Catholic as well as Protestant churches swiftly took hold and flourished and that especially the former acquired a significant amount of property. The Catholics founded the *Wahrheitsfreund* (1837), the first German Catholic newspaper of the land, which in the beginning was edited by J.M. Henni, later the Archbishop of Milwaukee. On the Protestant side, *Der Protestant* appeared for a while, edited by Georg Walker, and later (1838) an organ of German Methodism, *Der Christliche Apologete*, was published under the direction of Wilhelm Nast, which both had numerous readers in their respective circles. (9)

Wilhelm Nast, who was born 18 June 1807 in Stuttgart, was a fellow student with David Friedrich Strauss in Tübingen, where he studied theology, especially philosophy. In 1828, he immigrated to America, first holding a position as a private instructor in New York, joined the Methodist Church and then accepted professorships of classical languages at various seminaries. He organized German Methodism in Ohio, founded *Der Christliche Apologete*, whose editor he became, as well as the youth journal, the *Sonntagsschul-Glocke*, both of which were the official organs of publication for German Methodism, of which he is generally regarded as its father. His original and translated theological works are numerous. In 1844, he went to Germany as a missionary of the Methodist Church and worked there with some degree of success for this particular form of Christianity. He attended the meeting of the Evangelical Alliance in Berlin (1857), and sought to win followers there for Methodism. (10)

Nast, a doctor of theology and learned theologian and philologist, acquired a great reputation in the religious circles of America, and accomplished a great deal for the preservation of the German heritage, especially the German language. If he had not founded the German Methodist press, which enjoys a very large circulation, then the German Methodists, who prefer to read their religious journals and often only them, would have become fully estranged from their German way of thinking. And, it also might be considered that as orthodox as the father of German Methodism might be that his competent and thorough education at a German university with a teacher like F.C. Baur provided him with a scholarly and intellectual background that warded him off from taking a too extreme theological position in contrast to many of his American colleagues. At the very least, he remains an intellectual firmly attached to his fatherland and one who enabled many of his young friends to attend German universities, although aware that the same might exchange their more narrow religious views there for more liberal and mature ones. He is generally described as a man of outstanding character, who has attained the respect of his fellow citizens in every aspect of life.

Cincinnati in particular was an important hotbed for political newspapers. In 1826, the pioneer of such publications appeared: *Die Ohio Chronik*. This was a weekly that in the meantime has ceased publication. In 1832, a so-called campaign paper was issued for election purposes, published by Karl von Bonge, Albert Lange (later resident in Terre Haute), and Heinrich Brachmann in the interest of the Whig Party. On 7 October 1834, the *Weltbürger* appeared, published by Hartmann, whose editorial policy was directed against the Democrats. However, this as well as the name was soon changed, as the paper passed into the hands of Benjamin Boffinger, who changed its name to *Der Deutsche Franklin*, which was then dedicated to the interests of the Democratic candidate for president, Van Buren. However, after the election the Whigs succeeded in acquiring the *Franklin* again (1836). (11)

The Democrats then founded the *Volksblatt*, edited and published by Heinrich Rödter, who was supported in publishing it by several of the most respected Germans, such as Rümelin, Rehfuss, August Renz and others. Heinrich Rödter, born on 10 March 1805 at Neustadt an der Hardt, was occupied in his youth at the paper factory of his father. Full of bubbling energy, his apprenticeship years were very stormy. A short time of service in a Bavarian light infantry regiment at Augsburg, which he left as a Junker, did nothing to turn him into a philistine. Returned back home, he then began the study of law. However, the political excitement that reigned after the July Revolution in Paris (1830), especially in the Rhineland, soon took hold of him as well. He became acquainted with the writers Dr. Wirth and Siebenpfeiffer, and other leaders of the movement, such as Schüler, Savoye, Gelb and Pistorious, and was involved in the Hambacher Fest, and in order to escape the threat of a court investigation, he left his beloved Palatinate in summer 1832, and came to Cincinnati, Ohio. Soon thereafter, he moved to Columbus, where he became editor of a German Democratic newspaper. However, we then find him again in Cincinnati, where he edited the paper newly founded by the Democrats, the *Volksblatt* (1836), in which position he continued till 1840. (12)

While many German papers, especially in small towns, previously had been meaningless party publications and true copies of similar American newspapers, Rödter brought a higher level to his *Volksblatt* and paved the way to a better quality of journalism and to a more worthy development of the German press of his state. The opposition paper, earlier *Der Deutsche Franklin*, was re-named as the *Westliche Merkur*, did not battle with the same kinds of weapons, and so often dealt sharply with Rödter's paper, without however noticeably doing much harm to good manners. The example of German papers elsewhere hindered this kind of development unfortunately.

The *Alte und Neue Welt* and several other papers in Philadelphia and Pittsburgh, but especially the *New Yorker Staats-Zeitung* and the *Anzeiger des Westens* from St. Louis had already been appearing for a number of years, and had acquired a large readership by means of their knowledgeable, diverse, often exceptionally well written articles. Wilhelm Weber, himself a knowledgeable as well as clever journalist, whose style was always exemplary and who placed great demands on the press, in 1837 called the *Alte und Neue Welt* a valuable publication, especially with regard to German politics and literature. At the same time, he wrote of the *New Yorker Staats-Zeitung*:

This paper under its present editorship (Stephan Molitor) has the most political content, as well as, in my view, the most qualified political understanding of domestic conditions. It has shown itself quite influential in fighting for the interests of the working classes against the oppressive force of the monopolies and has actively concerned itself with exposing the work of the so-called native-born Americans against the European immigration. (13)

He also spoke favorably about the *Allgemeine Zeitung* from New York. This paper had earlier been edited by a lawyer, M.A. Richter from Saxony. Of the *Adler des Westens* he wrote that it was a good Democratic paper, but that it was better known for its good and honest intentions, rather than outstanding journalism. He even praised the oldest Pennsylvania German paper, the *Readinger Adler*, especially because of its correct use of German, which placed it far ahead of the other older Pennsylvania German newspapers.

If we add to the papers we have mentioned the *Deutsche Schnellpost* from New York; the *Anzeiger des Westens* from St. Louis; the *Deutsche Tribüne* and *Die Waage* of Paul Follen in St. Louis; the *Weltbürger* and *Telegraph* in Buffalo; the *Teutone* in Charleston; the *Beobachter* and *Freiheitsbote* in Belleville, Illinois; the *Westbote* in Columbus, which are among the most outstanding German papers in the larger cities, where Germans have settled in great numbers, then we cannot support the opinion of Friedrich Kapp's article on the "German Book Trade in the United States." He says there:

> Here so much might be said in passing that the great majority of the German newspapers stood at a very low level till the 1850s, and mainly dealt with insignificant gossip and personal scandals, but that since then a pleasant improvement has made itself known, so that today there are many German-American papers that are not only the equal, but rather many times superior to German papers in Europe. (14)

To be sure, he is speaking here of the great majority of German-American papers. However, the press of the land should be judged not in terms of all the papers, but rather in terms of the major papers of large cities. If one would judge all the publications that appear in Berlin, Paris and Vienna that call themselves newspapers then Kapp's critique would be just as relevant. And what kind of a grade would Germany receive if all the papers would be considered as part of the nation's press, which appear in the small towns and villages? We agree with the view with the views of Wilhelm Weber, which were expressed in 1837, therefore much before 1850, which he noted at the end of his excellent article about the English- and German-language press of the United States:

> It could not be otherwise that an association of German-language newspapers (which he had just discussed) would, with a few forgettable exceptions, be led by the best and most moderate principles and would contribute beneficially to the elevation of the German element, to attaining respect for Germans in the eyes of the Americans, as well as to favorably influencing Germans in the old world as well. When one considers the short time period of its existence, the lack of material and intellectual support, and the newness of the German element then one can only hope that given an equal dose of diligence and competition that the German-American press will soon take a worthy place in the journalistic world of the civilized nations. (15)

To a great extent Weber's hope was fulfilled by 1850.

The German societies of Philadelphia and New York do not belong to the period that we are discussing here as far as their origins are concerned, although their activities reach into this time period and were more active than in the three decades of the previous century. (16) Their original purpose of providing assistance and advice to German immigrants landing in the harbor cities was brought to life again with the increased immigration in the early nineteenth century. Similar societies arose gradually in various places of the U.S. In Cincinnati, the need was also felt for a German society to eliminate divisiveness and disunity, which had been the source not only of various kinds of misfortune, but also the cause of political powerlessness on the part of our people. A meeting was held at City Hall (31 July 1834) that was attended by more than two hundred of the most well respected German citizens of Cincinnati, which decided that the establishment of such a society was necessary:

So that we as citizens of the United States can participate in the political process
as provided by duty and law, and so that we can secure for ourselves a better
future by means of mutual support, and can thereby assist the needy and attain the
beneficial goals that would be unattainable by the individual acting alone. (17)

The main supporters of this meeting were Heinrich Rödter, Johann Meyer, Karl
Libeau, Ludwig Rehfuss, Salomon Menken (father of the then attention-getting actress
Adah Isaaks Menken), Daniel and Karl Wolff, Raymund Witschger and others. Karl
Rümelin, Dr. Sebastian Huber, J.D. Felsenbeck, Karl and Johann Belser and many others
joined the organizational meetings held from the 14th through the 18th of August.
Heinrich Rödter was the first president of the German Society that still exists, albeit only
as a beneficial society for its own membership.

The rage for militia companies had already traveled from the eastern states to
Cincinnati at about this time (1836). At the instigation of Rödter, there, therefore, arose,
the German Lafayette Guard, whose first captain he became. (18)

At that time, endeavors arose to secure the rights of the German element,
especially in Cincinnati. Rödter was elected to the City Council and at that time was quite
popular with his fellow German citizens. In 1840, he sold the *Volksblatt* to Stephan
Molitor and moved back to Columbus, where he devoted himself to the trade he had
learned in his youth, the manufacture of paper. However, the business did not succeed.
After returning to Cincinnati, he studied law, and was then elected to the state legislature
(1847-48). The law granting workers deposit rights on the structures they built, as well as
the law lowering the costs for the naturalization of the foreign-born were both suggested
by him and passed into law due to his efforts.

Although Rödter belonged to the Democratic Party until his death, he nevertheless
voted for the revocation of all oppressive laws in the Free states against the free Blacks
and slaves. He gave his vote for U.S. Senator to S.P. Chase, whose feelings against
slavery and everything connected with it were well known. He had a business partnership

for several years with the outstanding lawyer, J.B. Stallo, but then turned to journalism in 1850, buying the *Ohio Staatszeitung* and editing till 1854 as the *Demokratisches Tageblatt*. In 1856, he was elected to the office of justice of peace by a great majority, but died in the following year. (19)

Karl Gustav Rümelin came from an old respected family in Württemberg that provided a long line of competent officials to its homeland. (20) His father was employed in various businesses and factories in Heilbronn, where Rümelin was born 19 March 1814. After having attended the fine schools of his hometown till 1829, and enjoying private instructions in modern languages, he left the gymnasium to work in his father's business office. After several years, he was commissioned to a position in a business in Wimpfen. Early on he had already been interested in immigrating to America, which increased in 1832 due to the strong immigration from Würtemberg and Hessen, which climbed to an overwhelming wave as a result of the writings of Duden. (21) Against his expectations, his father gave him the permission to carry out his dream of going to America. Our young traveler made the journey from the port of Amsterdam in a trip lasting 87 days, arriving in Philadelphia on 27 August 1832. As he did not immediately succeed in finding an appropriate position, he enthusiastically took on anything that came his way, since he considered every job worthwhile. After some time, he obtained a position in a store that was owned by an Irishman and had many Irish customers, so he had the opportunity of getting to know them better, and broaden his experience.

Already in Philadelphia, where he arrived at the time of the presidential election, there arose within him a tried and true sympathy for the Democratic Party that lasted his entire lifetime. For him, Jackson was a first-class hero. In Germany he had already become an enthusiastic supporter of free trade by means of study and experience, and opposed to paper money and banks. In addition, he felt that there was an inclination towards Puritanism among the supporters of Clay and the Whig Party, which aroused a natural sense of repugnance to his thoroughly German sensibilities. However, in consideration of his youthfulness and his very brief time in America it is doubtful that the decisive stance he took on this had anything to do with any personal experience or a serious examination of the issues of the day. It was rather a matter of a certain indefinable feeling, as was the case with almost all Germans of the time. The name "Democrat" had in and of itself a certain enchantment for Germans. They found it only natural to connect and identify the well-to-do merchants, great church leaders, factory owners, who almost all belonged to the Whig Party, with the aristocracy of Europe. A philosophical evaluation of both political parties took place with Rümelin, as with so many others, only later on.

After a year in Philadelphia, he felt the urge to move west. After a difficult and dangerous journey (at the time, cholera had broken out on the steamer that traveled from Pittsburgh to Cincinnati and had caused many deaths), he arrived in Cincinnati only to briefly succumb to this dreadful illness, which had now overtaken Cincinnati as well. He soon recovered, found a position in a shop and immediately began to take part in politics and public affairs. In 1834, he was one of the co-founders of the German Society, and remained a member of it for forty years till he moved his place of residence several miles away from the city.

In 1836, during the presidential campaign, the previously Democratic weekly, *Der Deutsche Franklin*, passed over into the hands of the opposition. Rümelin was among those who were dissatisfied with this turn of events. He took part in founding the Democratic paper, the *Volksblatt*, whose editor was Heinrich Rödter. The financial sources among the Germans at that time were meager, but the enthusiasm great. The printing press was moved into the building where Rümelin had his business, with no rent being charged. He himself learned the mysteries of the "black art" of printing and when necessary also delivered the papers.

The regular deliverer was a baker, who also carried pretzels with him for sale. As Rümelin often said, the latter sold better than the paper did. At the same time, he wrote articles for the paper, and suggested the founding of a German university in America. Due to illness, he was not able to participate in the first Pittsburgh Convention, however. Rödter and Rehfuss as well as Rümelin took part in the 1836 campaign, taking to the stump, and apparently with great success, since Hamilton County, in which Cincinnati is located, and where there still was a Whig majority in 1834, voted Democrat from 1836 to 1840. (Among those responsible for this turn of events, we make special note of C. Backhaus, Dr. Rőlker and Bishop Henni).The *Volksblatt* later on became the property of Rődter, and finally of Molitor. It remained a Democratic publication till 1856, when the great majority of the German Democrats in the North joined the Republican Party. (22)

At about the same time (1836), Rűmelin joined together with his earlier business partner and did very well, especially by means of the sale of many German imported specialty goods. Part of his profit was invested in property. He also wrote for American journals at the time. He wrote of this as follows:

> I represented German issues, as it seemed ridiculous that we Germans only discussed these topics among ourselves, trying to ignite some enthusiasm for them. I felt that the Americans should also be won over, if any undertaking of ours was to have lasting results. (23)

In 1837, he married a Swiss-born lady, who had lived for several years in Switzerland, but had been educated in New England. She combined the American and the German spirit in a pleasant way and became his loyal companion throughout his life.

In 1843, Rűmelin sold his business to move to the country, but first took a trip to Germany. After returning to Hamilton County, he was elected to the Ohio House of Representatives in 1844 and 1845, and in 1846 was elected for two years to the State Senate. In the House of Representatives he was responsible for having the annual message of the governor as well as the reports of state officials published in the German language. His minority report in favor of the annexation of Texas, not because of, but rather in spite slavery, aroused great interest, and was widely reprinted in Democratic newspapers. His speeches on the method of taxation of the time, whose one-sidedness he strongly opposed, demonstrated a thorough study of economical questions.

In the years 1846-48, Rümelin turned to the study of law in the office of Van Hamm, was examined, and admitted to the bar as a lawyer. He continued his legal studies, but did not find the practice of law to be of interest. In 1848, he visited Germany for the second time and wrote travel correspondence reports for the *New York Evening Post*, edited by William Cullen Bryant and John Bigelow, one of the best papers of the country. These articles also made the rounds with other newspapers as well. They contained many new and somewhat uncomfortable ideas. Rümelin, as much as the well being of his adopted homeland meant to him, was not blind to its weaknesses, and what he thought, he always expressed openly. While he was in Germany, he was elected to serve as a member of a convention charged with writing a new constitution for the state of Ohio. He only received this news when the steamboat he was on landed in New York and the captain brought the most recent papers on board (April 1850).

In this convention (1850-51), Rümelin was one of the most important and effective members. It was his particular honor that he was responsible for adding an article to the constitution that made the arbitrary division of electoral districts by the legislature an impossibility. This right of dividing districts had been greatly abused by both parties, so that often a minority in a given county was made a majority by the artificial formation of an electoral district. According to the present-day constitution of Ohio, the division of electoral districts takes place only every other ten years, and in accordance with the U.S. Census, according to constitutional regulations. Rümelin also contributed to seeing this regulation against corruption being introduced in other states as well.

A secret group within the Democratic Party known as the "Miami Tribe" was formed for the personal interests of its members with the intention of taking control of the Party, and this was something that Rümelin energetically opposed. And in the process he made many enemies in his own party, costing him a position as candidate for Congress. However, it gave him satisfaction that his work contributed to breaking the back of this dangerous group. In the famous election between Fremont and Buchanan he declared his support for Fremont, as did many Democrats, but only because Fremont himself belonged to the Democratic Party. He did not want to join the Republican Party as such.

A trip to Germany hindered his personal participation in this campaign. The trip was caused partly by family circumstances, partly for business reasons, which he had to conclude as president of a railroad in Europe, partly also because he had been appointed by Governor Chase of Ohio to the position of commissioner for reform schools. His task in this regard was to visit European institutions of this kind and become acquainted with their administration. After he had accomplished this task sufficiently in England, where he got to know Early Derby, the grandfather of the present day Lord Derby, who was quite interested in making improvements for the already existing reform schools, he then traveled on to a tour to France to inspect similar institutions. He also visited reform schools in Holland, Switzerland, and Germany. He found the French reform schools to be exemplary models, especially those of Met tray at Tours.

A report prepared by him and signed by other members of the commission was then presented to the legislature. A law for the construction of a reform school for juvenile delinquents was passed, and Rümelin was appointed as one of its chairmen by Governor Chase, a position he resigned from, however, in 1859. We also note that in the years 1854-59 Rümelin was a member of the state bank investigatory commission, as well as a special commission to investigate the embezzlement of state funds. An extensive, very interesting report of almost a thousand printed pages, mostly written by Rümelin, was the result of this investigation.

Although Rümelin had already surpassed the bonds of strict party allegiance since 1860 and frequently voted and worked for members of the opposition, when he considered them more qualified for office, he could not make up his mind between Lincoln, Douglas, Bell and Breckenridge when it came to the question of whom to support. He was one of the very few Germans, who supported Breckenridge, since he personally knew and respected him, and preferred him to Lincoln given his view of statesmanship. In the meantime, he had grown tired of politics. He was of the opinion that ignorance of the true situation in the North and South had caused the war and that it was the ambition of leaders on both sides that led to the war. (24)

He then turned to country life. Many years ago, he had acquired land on the outskirts of Cincinnati, where he planted fruit and grapes, and imported the best kinds of trees and seedlings from Europe. This love of agriculture goes back, according to him, through many generations of his family. He was not merely a "Latin Farmer," but rather worked hard with the plow, shovel, and hoe. (25)

In 1865 and 1866, we again find him in Germany, where he brought his oldest sons to study at a university. At the same time, he visited Italy, Hungary, Serbia, and Bosnia, and published his travel reports in the *New York Commercial Bulletin*. From 1871 to 1872, he edited the historical journal, *Der Deutsche Pionier*, in Cincinnati. (26) Thereafter, he took his sixth trip to Germany, to bring his two sons to a university and his daughters to a school. He himself (at age fifty) attended lectures at Strassburg and Würzburg on his favorite topics: economics and law.

In 1876, he was elected to an honorific position as member on the Board of Control of Hamilton County for a two year term. That he voted for Tilden in 1876, as did thousands of Germans, who had previously belonged to the Republican Party, was quite understandable. In 1879, the Democratic Party named him to a position on the state ticket as a candidate for state auditor, an equally significant as well as responsible position, even though he did not share the views of the Democrats as far as financial matters is concerned. All Democratic candidates were overwhelmingly defeated at election time (15 October 1879).

Currently, Rümelin is working on a work dealing with a critique of American politics, which should be of great interest. We have already mentioned his extensive correspondence work for newspapers, as well as his legislative career. He also actively wrote articles for agricultural journals. A lengthy study in the 1850s dealing with the climate of Ohio was published in the annals of the Agricultural Bureau of Ohio. In 1859, he published the *Wine-Dresser's Manual* and in 1868 *The Wine-Maker's Manual*. His most important work till now is his *Treatise on Politics as a Science*, which appeared in Cincinnati in 1875, published by Robert Clarke and Co. (27)

The first literary journal of the country appeared in 1843 under the editorship of Emil Klauprecht. (28) Born at Mainz in 1815, he came to the U.S. in 1832, and settled first in Paducah, Kentucky, which is located along the Ohio River. In 1837, he moved to Cincinnati, where he opened a successful lithographic printing company. At the same time, he also got involved in the field of journalism. In 1843, he published a literary journal, *Fliegende Blätter*, which featured lithographs, and was the first illustrated German journal in the U.S. Not long thereafter, he became editor of the German-American paper of the Whig Party, *Der Republikaner*, and in the course of a decade made it one of its leading journals. In addition, he wrote numerous novellas and an historical work, *Deutsche Chronik in der Geschichte des Ohio Thales*, the latter of which goes back to the beginnings of the history of the western territories and states. It contains much interesting material, and obviously required a great deal of source material, but in terms of a clear, easily surveyed and chronologically arranged work leaves much to be desired. (29)

From 1861 to 1864, Klauprecht worked at the *Cincinnati Volksblatt* and then was appointed as U.S. Consul to Stuttgart, a position he held till 1869, when he succumbed to the unfathomable whims of the Grant administration that replaced him with Black gentleman by the name of Sammis from Pensacola, a barber by occupation, and, as was said, was not even able to read or write. Since that time, Klauprecht lived in Stuttgart and wrote for the *Augsburger Allgemeine Zeitung*. He also contributed literary essays from time to time to the *Westliche Blätter*, the Sunday edition of the *Cincinnati Volksblatt*.

Klauprecht is a very gifted man, who greatly stimulated public and social life in Cincinnati. Inclined to irony and sarcasm by nature, Klauprecht was possessed of a very lively spirit as most children of the golden city of Mainz are. He entered the ranks of journalism at an unfortunate time, when opposing parties dealt quite roughly with one another. He had taken up the unpopular side of the Whig Party with the wind and sun blowing against him. Particularly in Cincinnati, especially in the English and German political press there was such a rude tone that took delight in the most personal kind of hostilities. To these often mean-spirited journalistic attacks Klauprecht responded with full force and there is no question that as clever as he was that he soundly defeated all opponents on this battlefield. He became accustomed to avenging the slander of others by returning the same in writing.

However, in 1853 when a German editor attacked the honor of his family, he was seized by the moment to right this wrong and seriously wounded the aggrieving party by means of a pistol shot. Placed on trial, he was found guilty to the astonishment of the public, which as a rule not only forgives such an action, but also tolerates it, and he was sentenced to a year in prison. Before his sentence took effect, however, the governor pardoned him, to the general satisfaction of all. In any case, Klauprecht was active for many years in Cincinnati as an influential journalist, as well as a political leader of his party. Moreover, he is said to have administered his consulate excellently.

One of the editors at that time of the *Volksblatt*, and later on of the *Volksfreund* was Heinrich von Martels, whose life was an interesting one. Born in 1803 at the castle Dankern in the duchy of Arenberg-Meppen, he attended the gymnasium in Osnabrück, then joined the Hanoverian cavalry as a cadet, and by 1822 had attained the rank of 2nd Lieutenant. As Captain of the 6th Infantry Regiment he took leave in 1832, and accompanied his father and brother to the U.S., where they followed the call of Duden, and settled on a farm in the vicinity of Duden's farm. He himself returned in 1834, as his heart remained with a lady of high standing in Osnabrück, for as he tells us in his book *Der Westliche Theil der Vereinigten Staaten von Nordamerika* (1834), this city of the Peace of Westphalia had stolen his heart. (30)

His book mixed fact and fiction in the strangest way, although one cannot hold this against him, as in any case, he showed that he was possessed of a kindly nature. His enthusiasm for England's sublime King (the sailor King William IV) is quite effusive, but as another king has noted, excessive loyalty is a thing of beauty. At the same time, the author speaks with the same enthusiasm for Washington and the free institutions of this country and his youthful enthusiasms have now given way to a more mature republicanism. At the same time, a light-hearted, skillful style characterized this Fata Morgana trip.

In 1839, he took his leave from the military, devoted himself to philosophical studies, and in 1845 returned to America. He went to Texas, purchased a sizable tract of land along the Colorado, but thereupon lost it as well as a considerable fortune. In 1850, he arrived in Cincinnati, finding employment for several years at the *Volksfreund*, but then concluded his writing activity in order to again try his hand at farming in Clermont County. However, he then returned to the paper in 1860. He understands the classical languages, speaks fluently practically all of the modern ones, and therefore works very well in the position of court translator. Literature in prose and verse form has always been his favorite occupation and amuses him still at his advanced age.

Another productive author of scholarly works is the doctor of medicine, Joseph H. Pulte. Born at Meschede, Wesfalen, he completed his medical studies, and in 1834 came to the U.S., where his brother, a doctor in St. Louis, was well known and had come some time earlier to the U.S. Here he actively took up the homeopathic method of healing that had recently been introduced in America by Dr. Konstantin Hering. After he had worked for several years at the homeopathic academy in Allentown, Pennsylvania, he then settled down as a practicing physician in Cincinnati. In 1855, he published his *Häusliche Praxis der homöopathischen Heilkunde*, which appeared in English in London and in Spanish in Havanna, and was followed by other medical writings of his. For many years, he edited the *American Magazine of Homoepathy and Hydropathy*. In 1852, he became professor and physician at the homeopathic instructional institution in Cleveland. He also founded and funded the Pulte Homeopathic Medical College in Cincinnati, which opened 27 September 1872. We should mention that aside from his literary works, Dr. Pulte also was the author of a philosophical work, *Organan in der Weltgeschichte*, which appeared in Cincinnati in 1846 and contributed to the literature on the topic. For an analysis of this

work we must refer readers to a lecture by H.A. Rattermann, presented in Cincinnati (26.
December 1877). (31)

Heinrich A. Rattermann, editor for several years of the historical journal, *Der
Deutsche Pionier*, occupies a place of great stature among the German-American authors
of Cincinnati. (32) Born 14 October 1832 in Ankum near Osnabrück, he came to
Cincinnati with his family in 1846, where his father continued the furniture making trade
he had learned in the old country. The circumstances demanded that Heinrich take on
work soon after arriving in Cincinnati, but early on he used whatever free time he had to
thoroughly master the English language. After the early death of his father (January
1850), the responsibility for providing for the family fell to him, and even though he
continued to work fulltime, he still found time to continue his studies. A long period
without work caused him to give up his trade, but with savings he was able to attend a
business school, and became an accountant for a relative, later on becoming part owner of
a lumber company. After dissolving this partnership, he worked for other commercial
enterprises.

At his instigation and due to his indefatigable efforts, the German Mutual
Insurance Company of Cincinnati was then founded in the spring of 1858, and soon
became one of the foremost companies of its kind in the U.S., with Rattermann serving as
its Secretary and Director. Even the great work he put into this company could not put a
damper on his inner passion for literature and music. He wrote literary works in English
and German under the pen name of "Hugo Reimmund," but cultivated the field of
historical, particularly cultural-historical research, with great interest. (33)

Above all, he made it his task to vindicate a just appraisal of the role played by
German element in American history. With a rare kind of zeal, a true sense of
enthusiasm, he followed the path of immigrants of German origins back into the earliest
of times, and his research in this and related areas displays a critical and discerning
judgment. There is probably no book or pamphlet unknown to him relating to this field
of research and he made extensive use of the archives in Washington, D.C., as well as

elsewhere. He has been occupied with historical research for a number of years now, and has edited the historical journal, *Der Deutsche Pionier*, since 1874. (34) This aims to inform the reader in an interesting way about the history of German life in America in every possible area of the country. Since its appearance (1869), it has collected a rich storehouse of material that can be evaluated in its entirety for a work on the German immigration by no one better than Rattermann himself.

He published a historical sketch on the city of Cincinnati, several novellas, as well as a history of the American West, *Geschichte des grossen amerikanischen Westens*, which appeared in two volumes in Cincinnati (1876-77). He has the greatest love for music, is himself a good musician and was co-founder and member of the federation of German-American singing societies, the *Sängerbund* (1849), of the *Männerchor* (1857), and the *Orpheus* (1868). He is a member and one of the curators of the Historical and Philosophical Society of Ohio, a member of the Cincinnati Literary Club, a corresponding member of the New York Historical Society, and one of the founders of the German Literary Club of Cincinnati. (35) His famed historical research was facilitated by the fact that he possesses an important and valuable private library. (36) In the interest of his insurance company he has also made a thorough study of the law, especially in those branches dealing with insurance matters. (37)

Such an active and many-sided mind could not of course remain oblivious to politics. Early on, he was a member of the Democratic Party, working for it in exemplary fashion by speaking and writing on its behalf. After the Civil War, when there was much discontent with both of the major parties, he worked for an independent Reform Party and we find him as a delegate of the same at its convention in Cincinnati (1872), which took place at the same time as that of the Liberal Republicans. The Reform Party, which many of the most standing people belonged to, especially those from Ohio, drew up an excellent program, deviating only in one essential point from that of the Liberal Republicans, but did not endorse the nomination of Greeley as a presidential candidate because he was a lifelong supporter of the protective tariff, which the Reform Party had decisively rejected as a national policy for the country.

At least, Rattermann's political activity was now silenced for the time being, but came to life again with full force in the election of 1876, when he actively campaigned, writing and speaking on behalf of Tilden, who then as the Governor of New York seemed to the Democrats, as well as some of the Republicans as the most desirable candidate for President due to his battles against corruption and his successful attempts at reform.

Chapter Two

Ohio, Part II

The School Question in Cincinnati – Dr. Friedrich Rőlker – The German Reading and Educational Society – Notary Public Renz – Joseph A. Hemann – Stephan Molitor – Georg Walker – Ludwig Rehfuss – Ohio in the Mexican and Civil Wars – General August Moor – General August Viktor Kautz – General Gottfried Weitzel – Political Life – The German Democratic Party – The Battle against Nativism, 1836 and 1844 – The Democratic Party and the Germans – Festival and Demonstration on 1 May 1844 – Nikolaus Hőffer

The success that Germans experienced by strongly supporting the Democrats for the election of 1836 caused them to request some return favors in response. Above all, they insisted that German be introduced into the public schools as part of the curriculum. Already as early as 1836, a German school had been opened in the Lane Seminary controlled by the Presbyterians, the so-called Emigrant School, which was maintained by the Emigrants' Friends Society. The main leaders of this institution, at the head of which stood Bellamy Storer, a member of Congress and later on a judge (Johann Meyer was vice-president and Jakob Gűlich was Chairman of the Executive Committee) were the German-Pole Johann Joseph Lehmanowsky, who functioned as general-agent of the society, and F.C.F. Salomon from Erfurt, who served as principal. Lehmanowsky also established schools in Dayton, Ohio; Louisville, Kentucky; and New Albany, Indiana. The teachers of the Cincinnati Emigrant School, aside from Salomon, included a literarily inclined and cheerful former German student, Julius Weyse, and a somewhat eccentric personality, Julius Schwarz, son of Professor Schwarz of Heidelberg. (1)

As the Emigrant School was suspected of proselytizing for the Presbyterians and as the German Catholics had formed their own German school under the direction of Father J.M. Henni (now Archbishop of Milwaukee), where there were truly competent teachers like Dr. Rőlker, Moormann and Dengler, who later became lawyers, it was therefore decided after much discussion to request the introduction of German into the public schools that were supported by taxes. People turned to the school board, which immediately rejected the request as not in accordance with its responsibilities, and indicated that only the state legislature could provide the necessary assistance. The question was then sent to the state legislature, which passed a law (1838), according to which in such districts where an adequate number of people requested German instruction and there was a sufficient number of students that the trustees of school boards "may" then permit German to be introduced into the curriculum.

With this law in hand members of the German community then returned to the school board in Cincinnati, which again rejected the request, basing its refusal on the use of the word "may." Now efforts began anew and candidates for the election of 1839 for the state legislature were asked to work for changing the "may" in the law to "shall," so that the permission would be changed from permission to an obligation. The unity and the clout that the Germans obviously had at election times caused the Democrats to support this measure and the law was changed accordingly (18 March 1840).

In summer 1840, the first German-English public school was opened, with Joseph A. Hemann as principal, and Heinrich Pöppelmann, Georg La Barre and Emilie Frankenstein as assistant teachers. However, the problem of German-English public schools was still not yet solved, and encouraged by the 1840 election, the Whig majority, which had always opposed German instruction in the public schools, tried to cripple German instruction by transforming German-English schools into German-language only schools under the direction of an English-speaking principal, while at the same time dismissing the German principal. (2)

The Cincinnati Germans were not pleased with this turn of events, and a series of heavily attended public meetings were held, in which speeches and resolutions were passed strongly requesting their rights. The first of these meetings took place on 16 July 1841, and was chaired by Karl Belser. Eduard Mühl gave an excellent address in favor of defending the rights of Germans, especially as regards German instruction for children. (3)

The did not leave this, however, at the level of merely protesting, but rather appointed a standing committee for reviewing German educational interests and when they continued to find them ignored by the school board, they continued to press for their requests for German-English schools till they finally obtained their goal. The main agitators in this matter were: August Renz, Stephan Molitor, Heinrich Rödter, Ludwig Rehfuss, Pastor Seib, Emil Klauprecht, Eduard Mühl, Nikolaus Höffer and others. (4)

Their efforts were finally crowned with success; and the current German-English public school system in Cincinnati is more effective than in any other American city, providing German instruction for all grades of the school system, and this truly is the fruit of energetic agitation going back to this time.

To protect these so difficultly won advantages, it was then undertaken to obtain representation on the school board. However, this was a difficult task, because the 5th ward, in which Germans were particularly strong, still had a Whig majority. Dr. Rölker was chosen as the only electable person, since he enjoyed a sufficient number of contacts with Americans to successfully campaign for office. He was then elected as the first German representative on the school board of Cincinnati in 1843, and was elected in the following two elections.

Dr. Friedrich Rölker, born in 1809 in Osnabrück, graduated from the Karolinum Gymnasium, and then attended the seminar at Münster. (5) After completing his studies he served as a teacher for a short time in Osnabrück and then immigrated to Amerca in 1835, worked for two years in New York as a teacher, and then came to Cincinnati, where he became a teacher of English at a public school (1837). He held this position for two years, when at Henni's instigation he was called to the position of principal at the school of the Catholic Trinity School. After one year, he resigned this position to study medicine at the Ohio Medical College. At that time, some competent German professors

(Dr. Gross and Dr. Johann Eberle) taught there under the direction of the important scholar Dr. Daniel Drake. Rölker graduated from there and since that time practiced medicine in Cincinnati.

His position as an English teacher in the public schools brought him into contact with some of the most important people of the city, as well as the influential members of the school board, and when the Germans in the 5th ward recommended him for a position on the board, he was elected in spite of the fact that the Democratic Party, to which he belonged, was in the minority. On the school board he immediately was appointed the chairman of a committee for German instruction, and worked by means of his moderate and thoughtful, but nonetheless effective manner, so that the previously negative position of the board with regard to German instruction was considerably altered. The German-English school recovered and blossomed due to his indefatigable efforts, and by the time of winter exams, the results showed that students did better in English than those in the English-language only schools.

That was a triumph for the German element that filled everyone with joy, so that a public meeting was called to express gratitude to Dr. Rölker for his work. The German school was secured. He was particularly well equipped with all the necessary requirements for his position, as one of his supporters in the spring 1844 election had noted in an article in the *Volksblatt.* His re-election was an easy one, and even in 1845 when the German part of the ward was separated off and raised to an independent ward and the Whigs, who were in the majority in the ward, nominated General Findlay for the position, and the Democrats felt so week that they didn't dare nominate Dr. Rölker again, he was nevertheless re-elected to the astonishment of all, entirely without any effort on his part.

Rölker in the meantime saw that the status of the German language was not dependent on German instruction alone, but rather was in need of further support, so as to bring the seed to fruition that had been planted in the school. For this reason he suggested the founding of a library society, which then came into being in fall 1844. Dr. Rölker participated in the founding of the society known as the German Reading and Educational Society along with Rehfuss, Rödter, Molitor, Dr. Tellkampf (who left Cincinnati soon thereafter), La Barre (later on, the society's librarian for many years), and many others.

Rölker became the first president of the society, which then grew and thrived till the Civil War, when due to the pressures of the time, it donated its library of 4,000 volumes to the *Männerchor*, which still maintains the library for its membership. The large Public Library of Cincinnati, which holds more than a hundred thousand volumes, has in the meantime made this library superfluous and is no longer of importance for use. In 1845, the German Catholics also established a German library, which was administered by the German Catholic School and Reading Society. It consisted of 4,000 volumes and later on was given to the Catholic Institute.

The German Reading and Educational Society became ever more important and effective than being confined to the reading of books alone under Dr. Rölker's and later on, Stallo's direction (Stallo became his successor as president of the society). Scholarly lectures were held, including those by Stallo, Georg Fein from Braunschweig and five lectures by Franz von Löher, which were later published in book-form as *Des Deutschen Volkes Bedeutung in der Weltgeschichte*. (6)

After Dr. Rölker retired from his position on the school board, he was appointed to the important position of school examiner, a position he held till 1848, at which time he then visited Germany. He now lives in Cincinnati as a practicing physician. The Cincinnati Germans probably have no other person to thank more than Dr. Rölker for the introduction of German instruction in the public schools of the city. He was well qualified with a scholarly education and his practical experience as a teacher and his clear and calm manner were successful in attaining what others had begun with passion, but did not know how to bring to fruition. He was succeeded on the school board up to 1850 by the following: Heinrich Rödter, Stephan Molitor, F.H. Röwekamp, Johann Schiff, and Dr. S. Unzicker.

The notary public August Renz, according to all reports, was the first to speak out on behalf of German instruction in the public schools. (7) He was born 1803 in Würtemberg, studied law at the University of Tübingen and practices law thereafter. He came to Cincinnati in 1833, taking on the profession of a notary public. His poor pronunciation of English and poor public speaking abilities, including a degree of shyness, held him off from becoming a practicing lawyer. However, his notary public office was quite successful. Moreover, he was very interested in the political press, and was in partnership with Georg Walker, publisher of the weekly *Der Deutsch-Amerikaner* (1839) and later of the second German Democratic paper in Cincinnati, *Die Volksbühne* (1841-45). His active participation in all public affairs of the Cincinnati Germans was always guided by the principle of serving the public good.

Joseph Anton Hermann, the first German principal in the German-English schools of Cincinnati, was born in 1816 in Oesede near Osnabrück. (8) He attended the gymnasium in Osnabrück, and immigrated to America in 1837, first teaching in Canton, Ohio, and then coming to a teaching position at the school of St. Mary's in 1839. After passage of the law allowing German instruction in public schools, he took the exam for the position of principal along with the German travel author Friedrich Gerstäcker, who was staying in Cincinnati at the time, and then obtained the position, which h e held for a year. (9) When the school board tried to suppress the German program in 1841, and the Germans, as is reported, tried to keep the school afloat by voluntary contributions, he again took on the position as principal. In the following year, he resigned the position, returning again to his previous position at St. Mary's. Later on (1850), he founded the *Cincinnati Volksfreund*, the still existing German Democratic daily in Cincinnati, which he published till 1863, when he retired. He acquired special merit for instigating the publication of the historical journal *Der Deutsche Pionier*. He now lives in Canton, Ohio, and edits the *Ohio Volkszeitung*, which is published there.

We have already mentioned Molitor and Walker, both of whom occupy an honored place in the history of the German press of Cincinnati. Stephan Molitor was born 5 January 1806 in Cheslitz, Oberfanken, and in 1823 began studies in philosophy and law in Würzburg. (10) His cheerful and independent student life did not get in the way of serious learning and several years after completing his studies he obtained a position in the police department of Munich. The reasons for his immigration remain unknown, but in 1830, he came to the U.S. In early 1835, we find him as the first editor of the recently founded *New Yorker Staats-Zeitung*. But soon thereafter we see him in Buffalo, where he took over the editorship of the *Weltbürger*, where he remained till moving to Cincinnati in 1837. He worked there with Heinrich Rödter for a time at the *Volksblatt*, which he acquired ownership of in a year's time, and edited it then with great skill and success till 1863. (11) His legal education and experience in governmental service provided him with significant advantages above and beyond most of his journalistic competitors. He became acquainted with American history and politics and could discuss the contemporary economic and political questions with expertise that today would escape many of the otherwise so talented editors of widely read German-American newspapers. In 1863, he sold his paper, retired from public life, moved to his rural land holdings and then died in Cincinnati (25 July 1873).

In this long time period from 1837 to 1863, he worked at his paper for the intellectual edification of his countrymen for everything that he considered to be in the best interest of his people. In an obituary that appeared at the time of his death in the *Pionier* it was said:

> Only this much can be said here, that he exerted the greatest influence in state and local affairs, worked indefatigably for the formation of our German-American public schools, and never was afraid of fighting for the public well-being, as well as for individual rights. (12)

His friend Rümelin is of the opinion that Molitor exerted considerable influence nationally by means of work in the German-American press. He emphasized his business sense that created for him a secure position, without however throwing any wealth on the scale for himself, nonetheless making it easy for him to maintain his independence as an individual in the press. "We well knew that he appreciated public honors," continued Rűmelin, "but also that he attained them in moderation and with a goal in mind. He was free of chasing after an office. His striving after fame and honor were well known, but also that he did so within the framework of his work for the *Volksblatt*, a real man of the people, as is appropriate for the head of a Republican paper."

Georg Walker was born in Urach near Reutlingen in Wűrtemberg in ca. 1808, and was one of those persons, who clearly missed their opportunity in life. (13)A thoroughly educated student of theology at the seminary in Tűbingen, he had been influenced by the ideas of Hegel and Strauss, and intellectually moved away from orthodoxy. Like others, he probably could have become accustomed to a position in the homeland and worked out a compromise with orthodox faith. But an invitation from the Lutheran Synod based in Baltimore was sent to the theological faculty in Tűbingen, requesting that competent young theologians be sent to teach at the theological seminary in Gettysburg or to be placed in service as preachers. Walker was one of the young men, who were sent.

Arriving here in 1833 or 1834, he found that what was called orthodoxy in Germany was considered heresy here, and it could not fail but be the case that no use could be found for Walker, who dressed and acted like a German university student of the time. He was therefore sent to a small Wűrtemberger congregation in Tuscarawas County, Ohio. However, he also collided here with the Lutheran Synod based in Columbus, and after he became active in politics as a decided Democrat of the Jackson school, he decided to leave his congregation. He moved to Germantown, which is located not far from Dayton (1838) and founded the *Protestant* in partnership with Dr. Christian Espich. At the same time, he took over printing the statuary laws of Ohio in the German language.

He then moved the paper to Cincinnati, where he became assistant editor at the *Volksblatt*, which at the time belonged to Rödter. The *Protestant* then took the last breath of its young life, and closed down. In the same year, Walker took over the editorship of the recently founded political newspaper, *Der Deutsch-Amerikaner*, which after an initially successful beginning, then also too folded. Walker shook the dust of Cincinnati from his boots, and moved to Louisville, where he began editing a newly established paper, *Die Volksbühne* (1840), which was not able to celebrate its first birthday there, as after a while we see it in Cincinnati under Walker's direction. How long he played around with this paper remains unknown, but he must have realized that politics was not his field, and so he established a religious-political paper, *Der Hochwächter* (1845-49), which was more in accordance with his interests, and which he published with the assistance of his friends till his death due to cholera (1849).

With his knowledge and unusual intellectual gifts Walker could have been much more effective if it had been possible for him develop further, and become more acquainted with the history, politics, and legal system of his new homeland. So he belongs to the not inconsiderable number of German immigrants, who although they are well equipped with the right inclinations and knowledge, nevertheless seem to manage to close themselves off from contact with non-Germans, and for whom the American world does not exist at all. Insofar as they participate in German affairs and societies, which have as their purpose to contribute to the well-being, social life and education of the German element, they exert a useful effect, but as far as American society is concerned they only make an indirect contribution.

Ludwig Rehfuss took a much more active role in public affairs, and was a friend of Walker's, as well as a child of Swabia, born 26 January 1806 in Ebingen. Well educated at the university there as a chemist, pharmacist and botanist, he had held positions in apothecaries in major cities throughout Swabia. However, at the same time, he took part in the independent political aspirations and movements that occurred in Germany after the July Revolution in Paris. In 1833, he left Germany, most likely as he doubted that there would be political reform in Germany, and settled down in Cincinnati, where he opened a pharmacy, soon enjoying one of the best reputations in Cincinnati. He became an active member of the German Society, took part in the establishment of the

Volksblatt (1836), became an enthusiastic Democrat, and was one of those who took part in the struggle for German-English schools, declaring that those who did not strongly support them would fall at the next election. (14)

In 1836, he also took part in the formation of the Lafayette Guard and in 1842 became Captain of the same. In 1843, he was one of the founders of the German Reading and Educational Society, and on the whole contributed very much to the elevation and liveliness of social life in Cincinnati by means of his social talents as well as by means of his good fortune, which made his home a real social center. He diligently practiced his profession and published the results of his research and experiences in several brochures, as for example on wine and plant growing. He became a member of the Association for Natural Sciences in the U.S. and he hosted its members when a conference of some of the country's most important physicists was held here. The 1848 Revolution must have greatly interested a person like Rehfuss. He showed the greatest sympathy for it and actually one of the greatest supporters of the fund drives for the loan instigated by Gottfried Kinkel to support the Revolution. In the area of politics he was always independent. Not even fifty years old, he passed away on 31 July 1855.

The Lafayette Guard that was just mentioned provided the stimulus for the formation of other German civilian guard companies. Soon there were the following: a *Jäger* company, a *Schützen* company, as well as a Steuben, Kosciusko, and Jackson guard. Several years later these companies joined together to form a battalion under First Lt. August Moor.

August Moor was born 28 March 1814 in Leipzig, and became a student at the Royal Saxon Forest Academy, which was organized along military principles. (15) His interest in the military profession may have its roots there. In one way or another, he became involved in the unrest in Leipzig or Dresden (September 1830), was investigated, and imprisoned for a long time and then sentenced to eight months confinement. After being released there was nothing left for him to do but seek his fortune in America. In November 1833, he landed in Baltimore, and then went to Philadelphia, where he found work. He also became a lieutenant in the Washington Guard there under the direction of Captain Koseritz, and in the Seminole War (1832) joined a volunteer company, in which he became First Lieutenant. After the completion of his service, the company was dissolved and we find Moor in 1838 in Cincinnati, where he opened a bakery that he successfully carried on for several years. The Mexican War (1846) naturally aroused his interest very much. As the Captain of a company in the 4th Ohio Vol. Regiment he distinguished himself in several battles and skirmishes by means of his cleverness and bravery, so that he was rose from Major to First Lieutenant, and then to Captain of the regiment. Several years after his return, he was appointed to the rank of Major General of the 1st Division of the Ohio Militia, a position he resigned from several years later, as it left much to be desired as a military organization, and actually consisted more of staff than soldiers.

At the outbreak of the Civil War, Moor was one of the first to volunteer for service in the Union Army. He was appointed Captain of the 28th Ohio Vol. Regiment (the 2nd German regiment). Commanded to the army of General Rosencrans, he distinguished himself in a praiseworthy manner in West Virginia, fought under Hunter in the Shenandoah Valley and was considered one of the best and bravest officers of the army. During the three years of his service, he led his brigade, but nevertheless was appointed Brigade General at the time he left service.

His open, honest character, his opposition of all favoritism, which unfortunately blossomed in our army at that time, his lack of flexibility, and the jealousy of all foreign-born soldiers, which reigned in all the higher ranks of the military, although the President himself was free of all such prejudices, may have hindered his advancement. He should have been promoted to the rank of Brigadier and later to Major General after some of the first demonstrations of his military competency. All his commanding generals, such as Rosencrans, Averill, Brunside and Hunter, highly valued him and recommended many times that he be promoted. In *Sonst und Jetzt* Armin Tenner writes that:

Everyone recognized his basic value and actual merit and modest as he was, he didn't chase after the popular whim of the time and seek the approval of the masses. His name takes a well deserving and lasting place in the annals of the Union. His serious military presence, which could also not be denied in civilian life either, was considered by some as pride and vanity, but valued by his many friends, who recognized the noble kernel within the rough shell and knew how to distinguish distinguished behavior from blasé vanity. (16)

General August V. Kautz, now Brigadier General of the U.S. Army, was another outstanding military figure belonging to Ohio. Born in 1828 in Pforzheim in Baden, he came to the U.S. with his parents as a child. His family settled in Ripley, Brown County, Ohio, where they lived when the Mexican War broke out in 1846. The young eighteen-year old joined the 1st Vol. Regiment of Ohio as a private. He was in the battle of Monterey and many other battles and obtained a position as Lt. soon after the war in the regular U.S. Army. He was a cavalry captain at the time of the outbreak of the Civil War, but did not command a regiment in the memorable days before Richmond in 1862 under McClellan. He proved himself here as a distinguished cavalry officer and soon advanced to Captain of the 2nd Ohio Cavalry Regiment, later becoming commanding General of the cavalry of the 32nd Army Corps. His brave cavalry advances aroused great interest. He was appointed to the rank of General Major in the voluntary as well as regular army. After the end of the war, he returned to the regular army as 1st Lt. of the 15th Infantry Regiment. He is the author of several brief military writings, which refer especially to his service. (17)

Joining him honorably at his side is General Gottfried Weitzel, who even has been claimed by the native-born as one of them, but in fact was born in Germany. He was born on 1 November 1835 in Winzlen in the Rheinpfalz, and his parents immigrated to America, settling in Cincinnati. In his seventeenth year he obtained a cadet position at West Point and after graduated there with excellent marks in 1855, and was then placed with the corps of engineers as a lieutenant, something which only happens with the best of students. At the outbreak of the Civil War, he was already a captain, joining the staff of General Butler, when he occupied New Orleans and received the command of a brigade in the army corps of General Banks, when he undertook his misfortunate expedition up the Red River. (18)

Weitzel then joined the Potomac Army under General Grant, receiving the command of a division, distinguished himself especially in the operation against Petersburg, whose capture led to the fall of Richmond. He was the first, who at the head of his command entered Richmond at the side of Lincoln. An unusual meeting! The German General Schimmelpfennig was the first to lead his brigade to Charleston and another German general was the first to carry the banner into the mightiest Confederate bulwark that had been long fought for. Weitzel is now major in the U.S. Corps of Engineers with the rank of Brevet General Major. Weitzerl's birth is validated by the fact that he is a member of the German Pioneer Society of Cincinnati, which only accepts the German-born as members.

From our brief description of the German press in Cincinnati we can see how actively Germans became involved in the politics of the country. However, it was really only by the year 1840 that the German vote really made itself known, having gained considerable influence since 1836. Most Germans were by far, here as well as elsewhere, members of the Democratic Party. It was hardly possible to be otherwise. Even before nativism had risen its threatening head the Democratic Party had secured the support of the German immigration. The most liberal naturalization laws were due to the Democrats, especially going back to the Jefferson administration. In the 1820s the Democrats in Congress succeeded in lowering the price of government land, moreover also allowing public land to be sold in smaller parcels (40 acres) to actual settlers.

After a long battle, extremely liberal pre-sale prices were accepted in the 1830s, which made it possible for settlers to pay for the land with a moderate part of his harvest. All these laws had been struggled for with great difficulty against the opposition of Congressional representatives in the East, who mainly belonged to the Confederate and Whig Party politicians. Henry Clay, for example, worked as a member of the Whig Party so that settlers, who were not yet citizens, that is had not lived in the country for five years, could not enjoy the privilege of this pre-sale price.

It was often said that the Germans and immigrants of other nations were mesmerized by the Democrats due simply to the word "Democrat," and by means of them generally speaking about freedom and equality. Admittedly, many are fooled by such rhetoric, but so much is certain that the great majority of Germans and Irish knew how to evaluate the real advantages that accrued from Democratic measures. With their mainly meager means, Germans would not have been able to acquire such large pieces of land from the government, which would have fallen into the hands of the land speculators. Almost without any means at their disposal, they were able to farm the land, because as settlers they enjoyed the advance sale rights. And, recent immigrants in the West did not approve of the protective tolls designed to benefit the relatively small number of manufacturers in the East, which were endorsed and passed into law by the Whig Party.

The most glowing speeches of Democratic politicians would not have been able to hold the German population within its ranks for thirty years if not for the fact that their material interests led down the same path. The repulsive nativist movement that was so deeply sickening to human pride, which first got organized in the years 1835 to 1836, then began anew from 1842 to 1844, making use of murder and fire. It was looked on favorably by a faction of the Whig Party here and there, while at the same time the Democrats at least decisively opposed it and promised to protect the rights of the foreign-born in all its public statements. Therefore, Germans, who were still undecided, were driven almost by necessity into the arms of the Democrats.

As in other areas, the Germans in Ohio also got organized and united politically, and there thus arose in Cincinnati the German Democratic Party of Hamilton County (1843). It issued a manifesto declaring its own independence from the Democratic Party, emphasizing that it would turn its back on the Democrats if they did not take its liberal principals seriously. If the chase after appointments and malicious prejudice against the foreign-born should emerge in the Democratic Party, then the German Democrats would take up battle against those unworthy of belonging to the Party. In this programmatic statement, the German Democratic Party endorsed the preservation of the highest principal of democracy, namely, equal rights and full justice for all regardless of religious or political beliefs. It also strongly condemned the nativist spirit of the time.

The board of the German Democratic Party was placed in the hands of thirty members, and among its officers we find the following: Stephan Molitor, Nikolaus Höffer, and Heinrich Rödter. The German Democratic Party was active in many ways. Above all, it provided Germans with recognition, secured them full representation at party conventions, and protected German instruction in the public schools, which had often stood under attack. The German Democratic Party was particularly effective in the presidential election of 1844, in which the Democrats elected their candidate (Polk). German voter assemblies were held and political clubs and singing societies formed, and from this time on the German vote weighed heavily on the scale in Ohio.

The news of the victory of the nativist party in New York City (April 1844) and the murderous fires by a nativist mob, which burned churches in Philadelphia, were taken very seriously in Cincinnati. The executive committee of the German Democratic Party called for a mass meeting to be held immediately in the hall of Landfried's Napoleon Tavern (29 April) for the purpose of seriously discussing the current position of the immigrant citizens of the country.

The brilliant speeches, which decisively condemned the outrageous actions of the nativists in the eastern cities, reflected a spirit of decisiveness that always goes hand in hand with justice. The Germans were admonished to take united action and to boldly confront nativism. A committee chaired by Georg Walker reported the following recommendations: A committee should be appointed to inquire of candidates for president, vice-president, governor, and other states offices "if they approve of the principals and actions of the so-called 'American Republicans' (what the nativists called themselves), or if they would use all their official and private influence to oppose them?"

Furthermore, a committee should be appointed to send prepare an address to the Germans
in America and another to the native-born people of America of the country, and to
present them at a spring festival to be held on the first of May. Also, this public meeting
should decide the suitability of holding a general convention of Germans in Ohio on 4
July 1844. Moreover, the disputes and squabbles in the German-American press were
also taken into consideration. The following resolution relates to this matter:

> Resolved, that we, the Germans of Cincinnati, have noticed with deep displeasure
> for some time the personal quarrels of the local German newspapers, and we
> definitely declare here, that in the future we will consider that editor as the
> common enemy of German immigrants, who ever again gives rise to such
> antagonisms, since in order to gain victory against an enemy, we need to have
> unity more than ever. (19)

Other resolutions referred to the participation of the German militia companies –
also similar organizations were invited from Louisville and Columbus – as well as those
relating to the organization of the festival.

The details of the festival for the 1 May 1844, which is described as the most
impressive public demonstration that ever took place in Cincinnati, are above and beyond
our focus here. Pastor August Kröll, delivered the main address, which was described as
a masterpiece of eloquence. (20) The committee, which had been charged with the
preparation of the aforementioned addresses, presented its report, but it was resolved that
"in order not to spoil the festive joy of the day with the depressing memory of the
mistreatment of our countrymen in the East that these addresses be presented to a mass
meeting on 11 May."

The address "To the Germans of the Union" refers in its introduction to the crisis
threatening the country and its liberties by the emergence of a political party based on
nativist principles, as well as religious and political fanaticism; implores all well-meaning
citizens to do their duty by addressing this evil seriously, but appropriately; reminds

Germans to view the preservation of the free institutions of their new homeland is their ideal, not ethnic pride, so that they will succeed in their efforts and win the support of well-meaning Americans. It also calls on them to join the Democratic Party, which "forty years ago, without consideration of any advantage accruing to it, revoked the Alien Act and since that time has truly remained true to its principles, and has always protected immigrants and their rights."

It also mentions that there are also Germans, who belong to the Whig Party, but admonishes them: "to take counsel with their conscience and love of country to see if there party membership is stronger than their concerns about the welfare of the country and the interests of future generations in America. Let them stay with their party," the address continues, "if they can, but they hope remains with us that our countrymen will soon recognize that love of the new homeland should be stronger than the love of Caesar."

When we consider that Molitor was the author of the other address, "To the People of Ohio," then we are not at all surprised that, aside from its most convincing thoroughness with which it deals with questions from a natural and human rights perspective, that it also reflects a thorough knowledge of the political history of America, as well as a spirit of reflection and moderation, which characterized Molitor's manner of dealing with such issues. The address closes:

> We will calmly and dispassionately follow the direction the nativist movement is taking, and in the future our first and foremost goal as always will be in the best interest of our new homeland and the preservation of its free institutions.

However, to ensure that the German element would be represented in the state legislature, the German Democratic Party resolved at its next meeting (20 July 1844) that Karl Rümelin be recommended to the Democratic convention as a candidate for the Ohio House of Representatives. The convention accepted this recommendation, and Rümelin was elected by a majority vote in the fall. Moreover, the German Democratic Party also made the request, similar to that made in Pennsylvania, that public documents printed in English for the use of the citizenry also be printed in German, something which the state of Ohio has done since that time.

In like manner, questions were asked of candidates for state and national office "if they were for or against the government becoming involved in matters relating to the temperance question, and if elected if they would oppose the goals and activities of the Native-Americans as regards their political and religious objectives.

We have already mentioned the name of Nikolaus Höffer as one of the most important leaders of the Germans in Ohio. He was born in 1810 in Rülzheim in the Rheinpfalz, and arrived in Cincinnati in 1832, and was engaged in gardening and finally was the property agent and administrator of the extensive land holdings of General Findlay. He actively participated in all activities for the common good of Germans, held the office of city commissioner and worked for the introduction of German in the public schools. He was the first vice-president of the German Democratic Party, was often elected a delegate to local and state conventions of the Democratic Party and exerted an extraordinary influence among Germans, as well as Americans. Rödter brilliantly and enthusiastically said that "Nikolaus Höffer has his right hand in all political affairs of the day." He died in January 1875 and the local press devoted many extensive and honorably obituaries to him. H.A. Rattermann wrote of him in the historical journal, *Der Deutsche Pionier*:

Among all the pioneers, who were active in the field of German-American cultural life in our city since the early 1830s, he towered high over others by means of his clear insight into the realities of social and political life like a mighty oak tree standing over the bushes below. Although he had not enjoyed an advanced education, he nonetheless was considered a leader of the German element in the upper part of the city due to the wealth of his knowledge about local political conditions, and to a certain extent was also viewed as a leader throughout the entire city as well. If in addition to his natural abilities he had enjoyed a better education, he would no doubt have become one of the most important leaders of the German element in America. (21)

Chapter Three

Ohio, Part III

Pastor August Krőll – Art and Industry – Friedrich Eckstein – Gustav Frankenstein – Friedrich Rammelsberg – Samuel R. Pike – Germany – Franz Joseph Stallo – Gustav Tafel – Joseph E. Egly

In the last chapter mention reference was made to Pastor Krőll, who delivered the main address at the *Maifest* held on 13 May 1844. (1) Born 22 July 1806 in Rohrbach in the Grand Duchy of Hessen, he was destined for the life as a clergyman due to parental influences. He attended the gymnasium in Büdingen, studied theology at the University of Giessen, and then accepted an assistant pastoral position in Eckhardtshausen. The meagerly paid position on the one hand and the influential book that had just appeared about America in Germany by Duden, caused him to join Paul Follen's Immigration Society in spring 1833, which immigrated to America the following year. In cooperation with the physician of this society, Dr. Brühl, he went to Cape Girardeau County, Missouri, where they leased a piece of property and proceeded to farm it. (2)

In 1838, Krőll accepted a call as minister of a German evangelical congregation in Louisville, a position he held till 1841 when he was called to the pastorate of the St. Johannes Church, the oldest German congregation in Cincinnati, where he worked with great success till the time of his death (25 November 1874). (3) Aside from his pastoral duties, Krőll co-founded along with another minister, Friedrich Bőtticher (b. 1800 in Mackerock, Prussia – d. 1849 in Newport, Kentucky) the *Protestantische Zeitblätter*, a newspaper representing independent Protestantism in the U.S. Bőtticher had studied theology at the University of Halle, thereafter becoming a teacher at the gymnasium in Nordhausen and later a pastor in Habernegen, finally then coming to America in 1832. He may well be considered the founder locally of rational Christianity, which Krőll also represented with him and then after his death became its major representative. Krőll edited the *Protestantische Zeitblätter* till his death with great skill and devotion. (4)

In the history of American art, the name Hiram Powers, the creator of the *Greek Slave* and *Eva at the Spring*, occupies one of the most honorable places. Few probably would know, however, that this son of a Connecticut farmer, the apprentice of a clockmaker, owes his artistic career to a German sculptor, whose pupil he was. Friedrich Eckstein, born 1807 in Berlin, attended the Academy of the Arts in Berlin, where he studied under its founder, Johann Gottfried Schadow. (5) In 1825 or 1826, he arrived in Cincinnati, and in the latter year, established the Academy of Fine Arts, which he directed till his death in 1832 as a result of the cholera epidemic. His Academy did not survive his demise. Only relatively few examples of his work are known, including portrait busts of Governor Morrow and later U.S. President William Henry Harrison. However, these are of genuine artistic value and the former can be found in the state library in Columbus, whereas the latter is in the possession of Harrison's descendants. His great reputation as an artist has in the meantime been inherited by his aforementioned student, who is among the foremost sculptors in the U.S.

At about the same time, the two brothers, Johann Peter and Gotfried R. Frankenstein, emerged as painters, with the latter especially attaining an important reputation. His great landscape painting *The Niagara Falls* has often been re-produced as a lithograph and engraving, while his bust of U.S. Supreme Court Justice McLean, which was completed in marble by him, stands in the hall of the federal court in Cincinnati. H.A. Rattermann spoke of him during his lecture on "The Art and Artists of Cincinnati" at the Cincinnati Literary Club, noting: "His paintings demonstrate individuality in their conception and are connected together with lively sense of color, characteristics which was passed on later to his brilliant pupil, Wilhelm Sonntag." (6)

In 1838, Gottfried Frankenstein was the moving force and first president of the rejuvenated Academy of Fine Arts in Cincinnati, which however was only of short duration. Another artist, Friedrich Franks, founded the Gallery of Fine Arts in Cincinnati in 1828 and was later the proprietor of the Western Museum. It is noteworthy that the various early attempts at founding art academies in Cincinnati were undertaken by

Germans, as Franks was also considered a German. With regard to the accomplishments of these art schools it can only be said that some of the most important American artists emerged, including Miner K. Kellog; William H. Powell; the Beard brothers; Thomas Buchanan Read, the American artist and poet; and others. Rattermann says of their value in the aforementioned lecture:

> The artists of this first period in the art history of Cincinnati had come from the school of nature, and had only come to that stage of study in which one lends greater importance to reality than to the ideal. They, therefore, belonged mainly to the school of realism, if I am permitted so to say. Only Eckstein, who had studied under the famous Schadow, and who was therefore referred to by Americans customarily with the vacuous title "Professor," was an idealist. His pupil, Powers, however clung so firmly to realism in spite of striving towards idealism, so that the former is strongly reflected in all of his works. His search for divine inspiration results in his work appearing with an almost bland, icy coldness instead of glowing in the higher light of warm inspiration. His figures are as pure as snow and smooth as ice, but also as cold as both.

Like everywhere else in the U.S., Germans also introduced and took particular care with regard to music in Cincinnati. In 1823, there already was a musical society, the Apollonian Society and in 1839 a singing society was formed, from which the *Deutsche Liedertafel* arose in 1844. From 1846 on, the three German singing societies in existence began holding an annual *Sängerfest*, and in 1849, the first great song festival in the U.S. was held here, at which time the German Federation of Singing Societies of North America was established, whose musical festivals have won world-wide acclaim. They also laid the foundation for the building of the magnificent Musical Hall and the founding of the Cincinnati College of Music under the direction of Theodor Thomas. (7)

In 1831, the organ building workshop of Mathias Schwab was founded, from which countless outstanding instruments have been produced that proclaim the praise of German expertise in this field throughout the country. The workshop, the oldest of its kind in the U.S., is now under the experienced direction of Johann H. Kőhnken und Gallus Grimm, both of whom worked with Schwab in the 1830s.

At about the same time (1836) the attempt was also made to create the machinery for the manufacture of furniture. The discovery of the Woodworth plane machine caused Friedrich Rammelsberg (d. 1863), a Hannoverian, who was foreman in the furniture factory of Johann Geyer, to try all kinds of experiments in this area. Some years later, Robert Mitchell, who had done his apprenticeship with Rammelsberg, also engaged in this kind of experimentation, however, without any actual success. However, as he then inherited a fortune, he then partnered with Rammelsberg in 1846, and now the latter began to turn his ideas, which were based on practical experience and which had been held back by his earlier lack of capital and an all too great carefulness, into success. He not only succeeded in constructing a large factory, which exists today under the name of "Mitchell and Rammelsberg" and employs more than 1,500 workers (the largest furniture factory in the world), but also to the rise of furniture making here and in the entire West.

We next meet a man, whose name was considered to be that of an Englishman, or an American. Even very few of his neighbors knew that Samuel N. Pike, the builder of magnificent opera houses in Cincinnati and New York, was a German. (8) The son of Jewish immigrants by the name of Hecht, he was born in 1822 in Schwetzingen near Heidelberg, and came to America in 1827 with his parents, who first settled New York, and later on, to Stamford, Connecticut. In Stamford the young Pike, as his father had by then changed already changed the name (Hecht means Pike in German), received a good education. In 1839, Pike moved to St. Joseph, Florida, where he opened a store, which he ran for several years, then moved to Richmond, Virginia, where he opened a shop for imported wine. Then he moved to Baltimore, later to St. Louis, and finally to Cincinnati (1844); in each of the three latter places, he opened dry goods stores. In Cincinnati he married the youngest daughter of Judge Miller, and began a liquor store, by means of which he acquired a gigantic fortune.

When the Swedish nightingale "Jenny Lind" traveled across America, Pike was one of her most enthusiastic fans at her concerts and one of the great admirers of "her divine voice," as he was given to say, and decided that if he ever acquired the necessary funds that he would build a temple to the muse of song which would do honor to Cincinnati. (9) When in 1856 the construction of the foundation of this magnificent palace was begun, only a few people knew what the purpose of this mighty structure would be. By means of the financial crisis in the fall of that year, the construction was postponed and begun anew late in the following year and completed in 1858-59. On 22 February 1859, the greatest opera house, at that time, the largest and most beautiful in America and one of the largest in the world, was opened in Cincinnati with all the corresponding festivities.

It was an epoch in the history of music and theater of the city. And, as Pike's wealth swiftly increased, he began to build a similarly magnificent theatrical palace in New York, the Grand Opera House, which he later on sold to James Fisk for $850,000. (10) He had hardly begun construction of the New York palace when his splendid temple to the muses in Cincinnati was burned down by fire in spring 1866. The building was re-built later and is now one of the main attractions of the city. A huge land speculation in the vicinity of Hoboken, New York led to further profits on his part, so that by the time of his death in 1875, he had acquired a fortune of several million dollars.

Pike was not uneducated, was a great lover of music, and himself played several instruments, was well read and wrote a number of poems in English that were published anonymously, but which display more feeling than technical skill. The little contact he had with Germans and his limited ability to converse in German led most to believe that he was an American. It was once reported that: "A small society that Pike got to know was told by him one day that he was of German birth, and from then on, he began to speak more frequently in his mother tongue." In politics, he belonged to the Democratic Party, and but could not be moved to accept the nomination to run for mayor (1867).

In 1841, we find that there was a German society for intellectual enjoyment, the *Harmonia*, and several years later a Society of Friends for Social Reform. In 1845, a German theater was founded. The active participation of Germans in the American political scene did not diminish their interest in that of the old country. Many national days of commemoration were also festively celebrated here, including the birthday of Jean Paul and Goethe.

Just as in other cities, a society was formed to support the movements for freedom in Germany, and which sent over large sums of money to support the oppressed patriots there, such as Wirth, Seidensticker, Jordan, and the children of the martyr Weidig. At the same time, a mass meeting of Germans got together without regard to their faith or politics, and collected $8,000 for those in need in Germany. (11)

In 1848, the first Turner Society in America was founded in Cincinnati. (12) The revolutionary movements in Europe, especially in Germany in 1848, found the greatest sympathy with a population like that in Cincinnati. (13) With all possible means at their disposal, people tried to encourage and support these friends of freedom. The arrival of Hecker and his friends in fall 1848 was the occasion of a splendid reception, in which Americans also participated. J.B. Stallo presented the welcome address that was masterful in terms of form and content. (14) Societies were formed to support the revolutionary movements, and sizable sums were raised, but after the failure of the revolution were then used for the support of political refugees.

It is understandable that with the growing influence of the Germans, that they were justifiably recognized as being entitled to holding public offices. In the 1840s, we find Germans in the state legislature as well as in various city positions, and their number would no doubt have been greater, if their limited linguistic abilities had not hindered them in this regard. And, also the desire of German immigrants for public office would also have been greater were they concerned about struggling for their own daily existence. It required a longer stay in America to awaken this kind of desire that bears so little fruit.

We have already had occasion to make mention of the name of Stallo and the German element of Cincinnati and the entire U.S. can be prouder of no other man than Johann Bernhard Stallo. His life was not distinguished by any strange turns of fate. He never inhaled the air of a jail cell, and did not bravely escape some threatening powers, as did the Follens, Lieber and so many other Germans before and after him. (15) The new homeland gladly accepted him and the hard battles of getting established here, which so many and often the best of the newcomers had to face, were spared of him. He spent the greatest part of his life in the happiest of family circumstances, spared of the storms that so many people of great importance have to face. We do not need many lines to describe the course of his life. Once asked, how he had mastered so many classical languages and especially mathematics at such an early age, as he immigrated at the age of seventeen and immediately found a position as a teacher, he replied:

> There are no riddles in my life, or at least none for which there is not a simple answer. All my ancestors on my father's and mother's side, as far as I can trace them, were country school teachers. My grandfather, whose name I bear, was my first teacher. He was an honorable old Friesian (Stallo is not an Italian, but rather an authentic Friesian name meaning forester), who wore a three-cornered hat, knee pants, and buckled shoes till the end of his days. He focused on my education regardless of being more than seventy years old and rejoiced that I could read and do math before I reached the age of four.

Stallo's own father had a great love of mathematics and instructed him in this field, and took care that he was instructed not only in classical languages, but also, behind the back of his grandfather, who hated the French, studied the French language. In his fifteenth year (Stallo was born 16 March 1823 in Sierhausen near Damme in the Grandy Duchy of Oldenburg), he was sent to the seminary for school teachers in Vechta, which he could attend for free. At the same time, he had the advantage of enjoying instruction from the professors of the excellent gymnasium there. In a short time, his knowledge of classical languages and mathematics had expanded so greatly that he was ready for the university, but his father lacked the necessary funds. He said: "There was no other choice for me but to become another link in the endless chain of school masters in my family, or to immigrate to America. The thought of immigrating was near to my heart, since the brother of my father, Franz Joseph Stallo, had immigrated in the early 1830s, opening up the beginnings of immigration from the Oldenburger country." (16)

This uncle was also, by the way, one of Stallo's teachers during his youth, who taught him physics. He was a very eccentric man, who ran a good business as a book printer and binder in Damme, but could not resist his interest in physics and mechanics. He made several useful discoveries. He is ascribed responsibility for the discovery of burning the moors, the introduction of buckwheat farming in his area, as well as the irrigation of meadow land and planting the same with fir trees, so that fields where nothing else would grow turned into forest land. However, as it often is with autodidacts, he frequently got bogged down with fantastic and impossible ideas. His business was neglected, and he also came into conflict with the authorities due to his free-thinking political and religious views, especially because of his activities encouraging the non-payment of taxes and immigration, as well as the dissemination of inflammatory writings. The trouble-maker was jailed for several months, his press confiscated, so that there remained little else to do but immigrate.

In 1831, he arrived in Cincinnati, worked at first at his trade. From here, he began an active agitation by means of letters sent to the old country, which brought about a strong immigration in1832 from Damme, Vechta, Hunteberg, Osnabrück and the surrounding area to America. It was now that Franz Stallo thought about establishing a German settlement and a society was formed. Land was sought in Auglaize County and the town founded there was called Stallotown (against the will of Stallo). Just as Rome first consisted only of an area surrounded by a trench, so too did Stallotown at first consist only of a might oak tree with a sign nailed to it bearing the name "Stallotown."

Stallo made himself of use at first as a land surveyor for the little colony, which on the whole grew in spite of its location, which actually was unfavorable, but was then improved in summer 1833 by draining the land, so that the population then numbered about one hundred people. However, the cholera epidemic, which was raging that year in Cincinnati, also reached Stallotown and took relatively more victims than in the big cities, including Franz Joseph Stallo. The town, which now has 2,000 inhabitants, did not retain its original name, but later changed it to Minster.

Our Johann Bernhard Stallo immigrated to America in 1839. Provided with letters of recommendation from his father and grandfather he immediately found a position as a teacher at a private school. In this position he completed his first work of writing, a German ABC spelling and reading book, which appeared without his name. However, this work demonstrated already his deep understanding of the comprehension abilities of children. There had been an absolute lack of such a book for the lower grade levels, and his work soon became popular and appeared in many printings. At the recently established Catholic St. Xavier's College there was a need for teachers, and the directors had taken notice of Stallo, especially his knowledge of mathematics, and therefore offered him a position as a teacher of German.

This was a nominal job title, as he was charged with the responsibility of teaching classes dealing with the classical languages and mathematics, and to follow these subjects through various levels in the next three years. He spent every free hour studying physics and chemistry together with a colleague, whose specialties were those fields, assisted in this endeavor by the large library of the college. With all his innermost desire for learning coupled with a certain passion, he continued this study from 1841 to 1843 till he was completely satisfied that he had mastered these subjects. In fall 1843, he accepted a call to St. John's College in New York City, a position he held till the end of 1847. The study of higher mathematics lead him into a study of German philosophy, and in 1848, the fruits of his study appeared in his philosophical work: *General Principles of the Philosophy of Nature*. (Boston: Crosby & Nichols).

Even if his chosen occupation removed him from his philosophical studies, he nevertheless remained loyal to the field of philosophy. He contributed numerous philosophical essays to the most important American scholarly journals, particularly to the *Scientific Monthly*. His philosophical library, probably the largest private one in America, bore witness to the wide field of his research interests. On his return to Cincinnati, he decided to study law. For such a mature mind it was easy to quickly master the basic principles of law in terms of their widest possible meaning, including federal law and economics. Admitted to the bar in 1849, he distinguished himself in his new profession so much that the governor of Ohio appointed him in 1853 as judge of the Court of Common Pleas in Hamilton County in order to fill a vacancy. In the following year, he was elected for a regular term to this position. As honorable and highly respected a judicial position is in the U.S., it is nevertheless not that financially rewarding in most states for those who have the prospect of a prospering law practice. Stallo, who in the meantime had gotten married, retired from his position in 1855, which he had, however, fulfilled to the satisfaction of the general public and law profession and again took up his law practice, which he has carried on with great success since that time.

If posterity does not weave any laurel wreaths for mimes, then the same could probably said of those who became famous practicing law. The decisions of judges of high courts survive regularly and in certain cases are published in collections of judicial reports, but the words of the most eloquent lawyers, even as much as they might determine the outcome of important victories vanish with the winds of fall. Nevertheless, Stallo was able to gain attention locally and nationally by means of the addresses he delivered in the courts of Cincinnati, thus acquiring him an outstanding reputation.

The school board of Cincinnati had by decree forbidden the reading of religious writings, including the Bible, as well as the rule that a chapter of the Bible be read at the opening of the school day along with the appropriate religious hymns, as being contrary to the purpose of the public schools of teaching all children regardless of their faith. This action on the part of the school board provoked the great indignation of the Protestant churches. The religious papers saw Zion in danger and felt threatened by the prospect of atheism and Catholicism taking over the country. A court case was begun against the school board for the purpose of nullifying the decisions of the school board. Stallo was called upon to defend the school board, and did so with ravishing eloquence. Based on the letter and spirit of the law of Ohio, on the cases of higher courts, especially also on the grounds of equal justice for all, Stallo spent hours preparing his speech to convince all neutral parties, but not the judges, who were members of Protestant churches and were influenced by the church leadership of the city. Stallo particularly tried not to take sides on this issue as best he could.

In this speech Stallo opposed the claim made by many teachers of law, earlier often without consideration of the consequences, that the state is a Christian one. He opposed the view that our entire civilization rests only on Christianity. He demanded a sharp separation of church and state as being in harmony with the Constitution and the spirit of the time. He reminded the court that the church fathers had built on the legacy of the pagan philosophers of antiquity, that the age of the Reformation and the age of Humanism had been a time of a rebirth of the arts and sciences of antiquity, that our Declaration of Independence and our Constitution had arisen in a philosophically skeptical time period that had preceded the French Revolution, that Thomas Jefferson, who was considered as an atheist by the orthodox, had written the former, and that the old "pious heathen" Franklin and other like-minded persons had helped complete the latter, and that the fathers of our republic praised the "rights of man" by the non-believer Thomas Paine as gospel.

It is impossible to convey the incisive logic, the wealth of philosophical truths and historical illusions of this speech by means of excerpts. Its beautiful thoughts were matched only by its exquisite style of presentation. Stallo and the entire liberal-thinking population of the land had the satisfaction that the Supreme Court of Ohio, to which he appealed from the court in Cincinnati, nullified the verdict of the latter. (20)

Stallo served for seventeen years as examiner of the candidates for teaching in the public schools of Cincinnati, and later on, was on the board of trustees at the University of Cincinnati, as he took a most active interest in public education in general.

That a man such as Stallo could not remain oblivious to politics is obvious. We mean politics in the highest sense of the word. What is usually meant by the term was of no interest for him. With him it was always a question of principles. It was only important to him if you represented, or opposed his views. Party activities, the machinery and organization of a political party, in which public officials hunt after their jobs, the web of intrigue, the artificial composition of primary and election meetings, were all the object of his decided disregard. Only once did he allow himself to be appointed to an honorific political position, namely, as a presidential elector for the Republican candidate Fremont in 1856. He never applied for a political position. Ambition was foreign to him. As a tangent only touches a circle at a given point, so too did Stallo only approach politics from the outside when great questions of life were at hand, and when he did so, he did so tirelessly by means of word and writing.

He joined the enthusiastic liberal reform movement in 1872, but withdrew when the liberal convention named Greeley, in whom he could not see as a representative of his principles in the matter of the free trade question. On the other hand, he brilliantly and effectively supported the election of Tilden in 1876. Shortly before the election he wrote a series of letters to the *New Yorker Staats-Zeitung*, which consist of a veritable treasure of his rational and statesman-like views, which aroused a great deal of interest due to their beautiful style and content, and were widely reprinted in various papers.

We have often heard the reproach made that Stallo was too much of an idealist in the area of politics, did not deal with the realities of the situation, and therefore was of no value as a political leader. He never aspired to be such a leader. He is not a political leader, but rather a teacher of the political parties. There are already too many realistic politicians, whose main concern is power at any price and the booty arising from attaining it. One does not need a lantern to find people, the so-called practical politicians, who sacrifice their principles to others, or only confess principles in order to support others. It is therefore so much more a joy to find people that do not appeal to prejudices, passions, and the greed of the mob, but rather to reason and conscience, and who advance the notion that there is no other morality for the individual citizen than that which constantly calls to mind the basic truths on which nations must stand that consist of ideals to strive after, so that public life does not drown in the swamp of vulgarity.

If Stallo is a master of both languages in the courtroom, as a speaker, and as a teacher, then so too is he socially as well, a unique person particularly among the Germans. And this man of the exact sciences and statesmanship is at the same time a person who appreciates the arts and is especially gifted in the area of music, which he especially takes great care to enjoy and preserve at his home. A very attractive exterior appearance betrays to one at first glance that here is someone with some great inner talents.

In all due respect, there is no German in this country, who combines such all-embracing knowledge with such an uncommonly sharp mind, deep thought with such an appreciation for art, restless energy with a kindly informality, a correct understanding of the issues of the day with the gift of communicating this understanding in the most clear and beautiful way in word and writing. And what is most enjoyable about him and what consecrates his work is that no one has ever doubted the purity of his motives and no one has ever believed that his active interest in the politics of the country was caused by self-seeking purposes or for the satisfaction of his own personal ambition. (20)

Gustav Rudolph Tafel, born 13 October 1830 in München, arrived in Cincinnati in September 1847, worked as a journalist, and then studied at a law school in Cincinnati. At the outbreak of the Civil war, he joined the 9th Ohio Vol. Inf. Regiment, in which he served as a lieutenant, later becoming lt.-colonel of the 106th Ohio Vol. Inf. Regiment. He was elected thereafter to the state legislature, and lived in Cincinnati as a successful lawyer. (21)

Joseph E. Egly, born 19 February 1828 in St. Gallen, immigrated to Cincinnati in 1845 after having received a good school and gymnasium education. There he found a teaching position at the Catholic St. Johannes School. He exchanged the teaching profession for that of lawyer after having studied at a law school in Cincinnati. He lived completely within German circles, and became exceptionally popular by means of his *Gemütlichkeit* and sociability. Early on, he became active in politics, or rather was drawn into politics by others, who wanted to exploit his popularity. In 1853 and 1855, he was elected as a Democrat to the state legislature. During the latter session, he held a magnificent speech against the anti-immigrant Know-Nothing Movement, which had aroused the public, and which was printed in English and German, and fully established his reputation as a public speaker. Other addresses of his have also appeared in print, as well as political and scholarly articles in the various newspapers in Cincinnati.

In attaining other offices he was less fortunate, and an unlucky star hung around him after he had begun his career so splendidly.   He was a likable and talented man, of whom it is said that it was his misfortune of having no enemies other than himself. He passed away in 1873.

Chapter Four

Ohio, Part IV

Columbus – Christian Heyl – German-American newspapers – Jakob Reinahrd – Friedrich Fieser – Germania College – Wilhelm Schmidt – German Churches – Dayton – Canton – Peter Kaufmann - Seraphim Meyer – Cleveland - The Umbstädter and Wangelin Families – Wilhelm Steinmeyer – Eduard Hessenmüller – German newspapers – Preacher Allardt – German Social Life – Judge Wilhelm Lang – Johann Weiler – Johann Sayler – Karl Bösel – Germans in Ohio Politics – Judge Georg Rex

The capitol city of Ohio, so exceptionally located in the center of the state, owes it rise in no small way to the German element, which started settling there increasingly in the nineteenth century, beginning in the 1820s. One of the first pioneers there was a German, Christian Heyl, who soon enjoyed the greatest confidence of his fellow citizens. For fourteen years he served on the city council there, eight years as city treasurer, seven years as county treasurer, and fourteen years as judge of the Court of Common Please of Franklin County. (1)

Early on in the 1830s, Heinrich Rödter edited a German Democratic newspaper there. The still existing *Westbote* was founded in 1842 by Jakob Reinhard and Friedrich Fieser and is one of the most widely read German papers of the West. Jakob Reinhard was born in 1815 in Niedernberg am Rhein in Unterfranken , and came to America with his parents in 1833, settling down on a farm in Ohio. Educated in a guymnasium in Germany, Reinhard joined the law office of Congressman Moore in Colbumus to study law, but then obtained a position as a surveyor and overseer for the construction of the National Road. In 1843, he began publication in cooperation with Fieser of the *Westbote*, and purchased the materials of the printing press of the *Ohio Adler*, which was about to go out of business. Their business, which they managed with the greatest circumspection, blossomed and they soon became well off. (2)

In 1868, they also opened a banking firm, Reinhard & Co., alongside their paper in Columbus with Joseph Falkenbach and the well known Congressman S.S. Cox as a silent partner. Reinhard participated actively in state politics as a member of the Democratic Party, holding office from 1852 on, for more than twenty five years, as a member of the city council of Columbus, and was twice, in 1857 and 1859, the Democratic candidate for the office of state treasurer of Ohio, and also served for many years as treasurer of the Democratic Party's Central Committee of Ohio.

His companion, Friedrich Fieser, was born in 1817 in Wolfenbüttel, and attended the gymnasium there and in Braunschweig. He immigrated to America in 1836, stayed for a while in Baltimore, and then came to Ohio in 1839. Shortly, thereafter, he took over the editorship in Lancaster of the *Lancaster Volksfreund*, which moved to Columbus in 1841, where it appeared under its new name as the *Ohio Adler*. Fieser edited the paper till the fall of that year when while on the way to St. Louis, he met Georg Walker in Louisville, who entrusted him with the editorship of the *Volksbühne* that he published there. This paper was called the traveling *Volksbühne*, and moved in 1842 to Cincinnati, bringing Fieser along with it as editor. However, its appearance was short-lived, and Fieser then joined Stephan Molitor's *Volksblatt* as editor to fall 1843 when he joined Reinhard in buying the press of the *Ohio Adler* for the purpose of founding the *Westbote*. The latter was edited with great skill by Fieser and became one of the most important journals of the country. Fieser wrote a humorous autobiography of his early journalistic career that appeared in the *Pionier* under the title "From My Memories." For many years, he held a position as president of the board of education of the city of Columbus, by means of which he did much for the introduction and improvement of German instruction in the public schools of Columbus. (3)

In 1830, a theological seminary of the Lutheran Synod of Ohio was founded in Columbus for German- as well as English-speaking students, with which a preparatory school was connected in 1842, which by charter took the name of Germania College.

The dean of this seminary was Dr. Wilhelm Schmidt, the son of a Protestant minister, who was born in 1803 in Dünsbach near Kirchheim below Teck in Würtemberg. He received a scholarly education at the gymnasium in Schleusingen in Saxony and at he University of Halle, where he obtained a Ph.D. In 1826, he immigrated to the U.S., edited a paper, *Der Amerikanische Korrespondent*, in Philadelphia for about a year, and then joined his two brothers, Christian and Friedrich, as well as Dr. Scheurer and Nikolaus Joss, in establishing a German settlement in Holmes County, Ohio, which today is the thriving town of Weinsberg. In 1828, he became a Lutheran minister in Canton, Ohio, and in 1830, the Lutheran Synod meeting in Zanesville unanimously appointed him as dean of the seminary, a post he held till his death (1839). Dr. Schmidt was also the founder of the Lutheran Paulus Church in Columbus, serving it also as its pastor. (4)

In 1843 and 1844, other German evangelical churches were founded, and in 1837, a German Catholic one was formed as well. All of these churches had their own schools, in which German was taught and preserved. Since the 1830s, there were also likewise a number of German singing and debating societies, as well as German militia companies. In nearby Zanesville there was also an active German community life since the 1820s. There were German Reformed and Lutheran churches there before 1830. As mentioned earlier, the German Lutheran Synod of Ohio met here, and established the Germania College in Columbus. Since about 1843, the German Lutheran church there was served by Karl Aulenbach as minister, who became well known as a German-American poet, and whose volume of poetry appeared in Allentown, Pennsylvania in 1879. Aulenbach was born in 1813 in Homburg in the Rheinpfalz, studied theology at Erlangen, and became a minister in Schneeheim near Lahr. As a result of his participation in the liberation of Dr. Wirth, he was forced to seek flight, immigrating then to America in the 1840s. Another German of note here was Heinrich L. Korte, who held a position for many years as a judge of Probate Court; he was born in either Oldenburg or Hannover, and came to America in the 1830s.

Early on, an active German community life could also be found in Dayton, located about fifty miles northeast of Cincinnati. In 1839, Georg Walker published a

German paper, *Der Deutsch-Amerikaner* there, and in the same year a German singing society was formed. In 1841, another paper, *Der Freiheitsfreund*, was also published there.

Canton, Ohio also seems to have had an active German element early on as well. Indeed, Canton was the first place in Ohio, where a German paper appeared, that is one not in the Pennsylvania German dialect. It was called *Der Canton deutsche Beobachter* and was published from 1821 to 1826 by Eduard Schäffer from Frankfurt am Main. From the latter it passed into the hands of Johann Sala and in 1828 to Peter Kaufmann, but changed its names several times. In 1835, a Whig Party newspaper was published, but quickly closed down operation.

Peter Kaufmann, a highly educated man born in Frankfurt am Main, settled down in Canton in 1826. He edited the paper published by Sala, later on purchasing and the publishing it for more than twenty years. At the same time, he published annual almanacs, by means of which he aimed to spread Hegel's philosophy in a popular way for the general public. In his book, *Tempel der Wahrheit*, which appeared in German as well as English Cincinnati in 1857, he gave expression to his understanding of Hegelianism. Kaufmann actively participated in politics, was a delegate to the Democratic national conventions of 1836, 1840, and 1844, and was appointed by Van Buren as postmaster of Canton. He also represented Canton at the Pittsburgh conventions held for the purpose of establishing a German teachers' college, and was president of the last two conventions. He passed away in the mid-1870s in Canton. (5)

Seraphim Meyer was born in St. Gallen, and has lived in Canton since 1828. In 1876, he was elected as judge of the Common Please Court of Stark County, a position he still holds. At the time of the outbreak of the Civil War, he joined forces with the pro-war Democrats and joined the 107th Ohio Vol. Inf. Regiment as Captain, participating in battles in West and East Virginia up to the Battle of Gettysburg, after which he was released from service due to illness. Since then, he has returned to his law practice, which he has now been carrying on for more than a third of a century. The Gutenberg Festival was also celebrated in Canton, and in 1842 a Society for the Support of German immigrants was established. Funds were also collected there for Jordan.

If Cincinnati was the center of the German element in the southern part of the state of Ohio, then Cleveland, located at Lake Erie, soon developed into a similar center for northern Ohio. Like Buffalo, Cleveland's rise began only after the completion of the Erie Canal (4 July 1827), which connected New York with Lake Erie, and especially after the completion of the Ohio Canal (1832), which connected Cleveland in the North with Portsmouth in the South along the Ohio River. In Cleveland there were few Germans at this time (1832-33). On the other hand, by 1833, several educated German families settled in the area. The idea of settling in America as a farmer, without any consideration to one's previous occupation in life, was quite common at the time and only few well-to-do families settled down in towns and cities. Some sad experiences, however, brought these "gentlemen farmers" back to their previous occupations, or similar ones, and back into urban areas as well. The Umbstädter family from the Rheinpfalz was one of the first that settled about six miles from Cleveland. The head of the family, Johann Umbstädter, had studied law and became a widely sought after lawyer in Cleveland, who later moved to Pittsburgh, where he also enjoyed an outstanding reputation and was also active in politics. (6)

In 1834, Mrs. von Wangelin settled not far from the Umbstädter family. This very old family originated originally from Mecklenburg, where the family had lived on its estate Gross-Schwerin for several centuries. In 1781, however, Mrs. von Wangelin's husband had entered the Saxon army, and participated in the Saxon service with Napoleon, and had returned from the Russian campaign in terrible physical condition. He was released from service, and passed away in 1824. The two oldest sons were both lieutenants in the 37th Prussian Inf. Regiment before their immigration to America. Hugo, one of the younger sons, moved several years later to Illinois. The other brothers remained with varying fates in Ohio, some also moved on later to Illinois as well.

Other well educated German families settled in the vicinity of the Wangelin farm (one of the sons had also acquired a farm), and among them, two are especially noteworthy, as the heads of them attained highly respected and influential positions. Both were political refugees of the year 1833: Wilhelm Steinmeyer, a minister and Eduard Hessenmüller, a lawyer. Both had used their time well at a university, both had passed their state exams, and both would have had the best prospects if they had not participated more or less in the revolutionary movements of 1832-33. However, their personal liberty was of the utmost importance to them. They did not want to spend the best years of their life behind iron bars, so with together with their young wives, who shared their fates, they hurried to our shores.

In 1836, Steinmeyer left the farm he had co-owned with Hessenmller to take a position as a minister at a small German congregation in Cleveland. He was a man of exceptional speaking abilities with a very kindly nature, and therefore was able to expand his congregation. He contributed greatly to the advancing friendship and unity amongst the Cleveland Germans. In like manner, he participated in the Pittsburgh convention held for the purpose of establishing a German teachers' college. In 1838, he received an amnesty from the government in Braunschweig and returned to Germany, where he obtained the highest possible position in his church.

The Hessenmüller family also was not content to remain indefinitely on the farm. He had been an especially light-hearted student in Göttingen and Jena. His cheerfully sanguine nature, his almost naïve openness, his honesty and his sense of honor made him especially popular with the *Burschenschaften*, and he had fully enjoyed the charms of life as a student. No wonder that farm life did not suit him, and that he sought a better, more socially, and intellectually stimulating position. In 1840, he left the farm and moved to Cleveland, where he again took up the practice of law. It was easy for him to get to know the local laws, and after a period of studying law at the office of a lawyer, he was admitted to the bar as a lawyer.

From then on, Hessenmüller actively participated in politics. As a Democrat, he led the Germans in battle against the Whig Party, nevertheless remaining loyal to the Union, and not being able to decide to join the Republicans. All of his aspirations, however, aimed to elevate the status of Germans in the eyes of their fellow citizens and to work for their well-being. He wrote a small work in German on the administration of justice in the U.S. and in order to acquaint his countrymen with American institutions, he translated not only the U.S. Constitution, the state constitution, but also the statues and regulations of the city of Cleveland, and published this in book-form. He also was a co-founder of a German beneficial society, and here it might be noted that a German society had already been formed earlier in Cleveland (22 February 1836). In 1843, he was elected justice of the peace, and held this office, even during the worst times of the anti-immigrant Know-Nothing movement, for more than twenty-five years. After he retired from this position, he held the important position of postmaster for four years.

His powerful, independent administration of these offices and his irreproachable honesty must have contributed to elevating the status of the Germans in Cleveland, as well winning regard intellectually as well. In 1847, he founded in partnership with Ludwig von Wangelin, son of the aforementioned Mrs. von Wangelin, a German newspaper, the *Germania*. This journal fought for the principles of the Democratic Party, but concentrated especially on promoting the interests of the Cleveland Germans, and deserves praise for bringing about the movement supporting the introduction of German instruction into the public schools of Cleveland. In 1850, Hessenmüller retired from the editorship of this paper. He was born in 1811 in Braunschweig, and even in his age, makes an impressive appearance, a Teutonic figure taller than most people. In spite of his in-depth involvement in American politics, he nonetheless preserved his original, fresh, cheerful, and tough mindset. He is one of the best kinds of a real and genuine German-American.

In all these undertakings Hessenmüller was greatly supported by Dr. W. Meyer, a very well educated physician, as well as Pastor Allardt, who had taken Steinmeyer's position at the German Protestant church. Of Allardt it is said that he was a very knowledgeable theologian, on the whole a very well educated man, a man without fault, and of fine morals. Music was also attended to, and Allardt's wife gave music lessons for Americans. At the same time 1840), a German choir was organized that made its first public appearance on 4 July. Flower and vegetable gardens were introduced by Germans and found great approval with Americans.

Here as well as elsewhere, where Germans settled in sufficient numbers, German social life emerged, including their festivities (the Christmas celebration was quite unknown in the early 1830s), outside activities, musical enjoyments, and their quite noticeable influence on social customs. The later massive immigration of Germans, including many from the ranks of the German intelligentsia, which would be sorely missed by the fatherland, ensured that the activities of their predecessors were not lost, but were brought to greater fruition.

If we look at other parts of Ohio, where Germans made their presence known, then we of course come across Wilhelm Lang in Tiffin in Seneca County. He was born in 1811 in the canton of Winweiler in the Rheinpfalz, the son of a forester. First planning to become a teacher, he attended the school in Kaiserlautern, and later the gymnasium in Zweibrücken, but then decided to learn a trade, therefore went to his uncle, a lathe operator, to study with him as an apprentice. His father, a man of independent view, feared harassment from the government, and decided to immigrate to America in1833. Wilhelm, who was of military service age, could not get a passport for immigration, but finally to flee across the border after going through several adventurous experiences, and then joined the immigrant group he parents were with.

After landing in Baltimore, the family went to Tiffin in northwestern Ohio, where relatives awaited them and where his father purchased a farm nearby. Wilhelm worked as a cabinet-maker and a carpenter and made it through some hard times. Coincidentally, he got to know a lawyer, who after learning that he knew French, Latin, and could speak English tolerably well, encouraged him to study law. He joined the office of a well known lawyer so as to study the field theoretically and practically and after a couple of years was admitted to the bar as a lawyer. In Tiffin, a quite lively area as well as county

seat of Seneca County, he opened a successful law practice. He was elected twice as

county attorney, in 1855 and 1857, and in 1859 to the position of secretary to the court,

and this after having served as mayor in the 1840s. Politics was always of great interest to

him. In 1848, he published a Democratic campaign paper, *Der Tiffin Adler*. Bilingual in

German and English, he was a good public speaker, and as result sought after by his

party. An enthusiastic supporter of Stephan A. Douglas, he worked indefatigably on his

behalf in the hotly contested election of 1860. In 1861 and 1863, he was elected to the

state senate representing Seneca, Wyandot and Crawford counties.

By this time, the Democratic Party in the legislature had diminished down to a

small group, and it required Lang to small amount of firmness and courage to swim

against the current at a time when the German element was almost unanimous in its

support of the Republican Party. In 1865, he was nominated by his party as a candidate

for the office of vice-governor, but was defeated, although he got more votes than his

other fellow party members, but then this was readily understandable given the

Republican majority of the time. Elected to the position as judge of the guardian and

estate court (1866), he then held this important position for six years to the general

satisfaction of voters. In 1873, he was elected to the responsible position of treasurer of

his country. Since completing his term (1875), he has lived in retirement at his villa

Weidenthal, located about a mile from Tiffin. A considerable library, mostly of judicial

and philosophical works in English, French, and German, as well as the classics, provides

him with the opportunity of remaining intellectual fresh. It hardly needs to be said that

Judge Lang no doubt is a man of great knowledge and exceptional understanding and is

possessed of an honorable and kindly nature since he has often received the trust of the

people at election time. The many important offices held by means of election bear ample

witness of this fact.

Johann Weiler settled in Mansfield in Richland County in 1819. Born in Herisau

in the canton Appenzell, Switzerland, he was born in 1780 and immigrated to America in

1816. Weiler was one of the main instigators for the construction of the Atlantic and

Great Western Railway, with which he acquired a great fortune in the course of his life as one of the major shareholders. When the construction of the railway was begun, the old German gentleman was granted the privilege of doing the ground-breaking. For many years, he was a highly respected person in Richland and surrounding counties, especially among Americans. He acquired his good reputation by means of his absolute honesty and his modest lifestyle. Through him, the German element in the Mansfield are acquired great influence, so that even in the times of the temperance movement in 1874, a German, Johann Bernhard Netscher from Dieburg in Hessen-Darmstadt, who had come to town in 1847, was repeatedly elected as mayor of Mansfield, although the German element there was relatively small.

East of Cincinnati in Preble County a man settled early on, who played an important role in Ohio politics, and whose family, which enjoyed a good statewide reputation. We refer here to Johann Sayler. Born on a farm near Ludwigshafen along the Ueberlinger Lake in Baden about 1780, he immigrated to America in 1805. He first farmed in Pennsylvania, and then moved to Preble County in 1812, where he also took up farming. He became interested in politics early on, and as he had became acquainted with English language and literature, especially appreciating the classical English authors, he soon became a well known personality in the county. In 1820, he was elected to the state legislature. In 1824, he supported William H. Crawford for the presidency against Jackson and Clay. Crawford was the leader of a group of Democrats, which today would be considered radical. It might best be said that Crawford was the nominee of the Democratic caucus in Congress, which previously been responsible for nominating presidential candidates. He was the favorite of the machine politicians, as they would be called today. Crawford failed and Sayler burnt his bridges with the Jackson crowd, so that for a long time he was without influence. In 1834, these divisions had completely disappeared. All Democrats were now supporters of Old Hickory. Sayler was elected twice to the state house of representatives. In 1837-38, he was candidates for the state sensate, but since Preble County formed an electoral district with two other counties, his candidacy failed. However, in 1839, he was elected senator. Sayler was the leader of his party in his county and remained the same till his death in 1844.

In 1826, he laid out the town of Ludwigsburg in the northeastern part of Preble County, a name one would have to take with a grain of salt as there was no harbor there. We also mention his son here, Johann Sayler, Jr., who also was a staunch Democratic politician, and one of his grandsons, Milton Sayler, who was born in 1821 in Lewisburg, who was elected to several terms as a member of Congress from the first district of Ohio, after having served in the Ohio House of Representatives from 1861 to 1863. He is a splendid lawyer and received part of his legal education in Heidelberg. Before becoming a lawyer, he served as a professor of literature and history at several colleges, and is completely fluent in German.

In Auglaize County, about 120 miles north of Cincinnati, several German families settled down in 1832, founding New Bremen. Karl Bösel, who came to America in 1833, had relatives there and settled on a farm in the area. Born 1 February 1814, he belonged to the many immigrants, who left their beautiful home in the Rheinpfalz due to their dissatisfaction with the political and economic conditions there. Farming did not appeal to him, however. He, therefore, opened a small business in New Bremen, and he gradually succeeded in doing well there, so that in the course of time, he opened a bank and currency exchange. In the years 1863-65 and 1866-67, he was elected as a member of the House of Representatives and to the senate thereafter, 1868-71. Currently, he is a member and president of the public institutions of charity for Ohio. (7)

It would require too much space to list all those Germans, who immigrated before 1850 and held important public offices in the state of Ohio. However, we might mention Philipp V. Herzing, born in 1809 in Karlstadt in the Rheinpfalz. He came to America in 1834, and lives at St. Mary's in Mercer County. From 1865 to 1874, he was member of the state board of public buildings for the state of Ohio. Georg Rex, born in 1815 in Pyrmont, arrived with his parents in America in 1819, and the settled in Wooster in Wayne County. He studied law and was elected to the supreme court of Ohio. Johann Bettelon, born 1829 in Steinweiler in the Rheinpfalz, arrived in Dayton in 1839, and was elected to the state house of representatives (1869-70). Joseph Heinrich Böhmer from

Damme in Oldenburg, was born early in the century, and arrived in Fort Jennings in Putnam County in 1834 as a school teacher. He served as a state representative (1855-57, 1863-65, 1867-68), and passed away, held in high regard, in 1868.

Other members of the state legislature were: Heinrich Brachmann, Johann M. Braunschweig, Leopold Burkhardt, Johann Joseph Dobmeyer, G.F. Göbel, Micahel Göpper, Ernst F. Kleinschmitt, Ferdinand Klimper, Johann Schiff, Heinrich Warnking, and Jakob Wolf, all of whom came from Cincinnati. Johann Mesloh came from New Bremen, Karl Oesterlen from Hancock County, Johann Seitz from Tiffin, and Johann Zumstein from Hamilton County.

Chapter Five

Kentucky

Kentucky – Louisville – German Churches – Johann H. Rőpke – G. W. Barth – Johann Schmidt – Phillip Tomppert – The German Press of Louisville – Germans and the Democratic Party – Nativism – Bloody Scenes at Election Time – German Militia Companies – Interest in Events in Germany – German Singing Societies – Other Cities of Kentucky

As a rapidly rising center of business and industry, Louisville, located at the falls of the Ohio River, naturally became one of the most attractive places for Germans to settle in Kentucky. While it had a population of only about 5,000 in 1820, by 1832, it had risen to more than 10,000, and by 1848, had surpassed 40,000. (1)

The oldest German congregation was Protestant, but its church was constructed only in 1841, while the Catholics, who had a congregation as early as 1837, constructed the Boniface Church in 1838. The Germans of Louisville occupied an important place in the trade and commercial ranks already by the early 1830s/40s, of whom we can only mention a few names: Schodt and Laval; J.H. Schroeder, of whom it is said that he is the benefactor of every noble cause, as well as the arts; Johann H. Roepke rose from the deepest poverty and was president of an insurance company and was honored with some of the highest positions by his fellow citizens; Georg W. Barth, merchant farmer, who raised a voluntary regiment in 1861 and with it entered into the 28th Kentucky Regiment. (2)

Advancing to the rank of Major, Barth led the regiment at the battle of Kennesaw Mountain in Georgia, distinguished himself at Peachtree Creek, where he and his regiment came without orders to the assistance of a beaten brigade, and enabled it to re-group, and then drive back the foe. He also distinguished himself equally towards the end of the war at Franklin and Nashville in the bloody battles against Hood. He was appointed Brevet. Col. at the end of the war. (3)

In 1839, Johann Schmidt, son of the former mayor of Bremen (d. 1839), who had been ambassador for four free cities at the Bundestag until it was dissolved, came to Louisville, after having been educated to become a merchant at the Bremen trade school and at the Komptoir of the Bremen house of Kalten. In Louisville, he and Theodor Schwarz formed a commercial partnership, and opened a tobacco business, which became the foundation of the present day tobacco trade of Louisville. They were responsible for being the first to bring tobacco from Kentucky, Tennessee, Indiana, and Illinois to market in Europe, all of which became so popularly well known in Europe as Kentucky tobacco. Since they began their business, the tobacco trade of Louisville has increased ten-fold. They likewise were the first to bring pickled beef on to the market in Europe. Both formed the first German bank in Louisville in 1855.

In 1844, Schmidt was appointed to serve as the Bavarian consul, and in time became the consul for all the German states, with the exception of Prussia, which was a position held by another widely respected citizen of Louisville, Julius von Borries, who served in this capacity for many years. Schmidt often traveled to England and Germany, partly for business purposes, but also for reasons of health. He died during his trip to Germany on 8 August 1871 after having an operation there. (4)

Schmidt was just like his industrious and outstanding father, although he h ad not been trained or educated to become a statesman, and was not active in local politics. However, he was a very enterprising and honorable businessman with an always open heart and hand and was always ready to be of assistance to others. He greatly sympathized with Germany, its greatness, and its unification, and like many Germans here, contributed generously to the surviving families of German soldiers, as well as to the wounded from the Franco-Prussian War.

In 1836, Philipp Tomppert, a man of significant influence, came to Louisville. We find him often as an active participant of public meetings held for various purposes. As he belonged to the Democratic Party, he naturally did not have a chance of getting elected in Louisville, where the Whigs held the upper hand. And after they were replaced by the rough and violent Know-Nothing Party, Louisville suffered for many years under its yoke, so that no German, regardless of party affiliation, had any chance of getting elected. (5)

After the downfall of the Know-Nothings, Tomppert was one of the first to attain a position of trust, and was often elected mayor, beginning in 1856, at which time Louisville had more than 100,000 inhabitants, which in itself was proof that Tomppert held the highest regard of the citizenry.

As far as the German-American press is concerned, the first publication was the *Volksbühne*, edited by Georg Walker, and which first appears in 1841. It was printed in a very insignificant place, and the editor also served as the printer. A visitor of Louisville, who worked at the time with the paper, reported that: "The newspaper was written, set, and printed from a philosophical point of view. It was democratic in its orientation, but independent in every other way, and did not allow itself to be slavishly regimented in any way. Even the format itself was not a predetermined thing, but conformed to the kind of paper being used, and which was the easiest to get hold of. The date of publication stood on the masthead of the paper, but seldom matched the date it actually appeared." After a year of publication, this first newspaper sailed by steamboat up the Ohio River to Cincinnati. (6)

In 1844, Louisville received another German-American newspaper, *Der Beobachter am Ohio*, edited by Heinrich Beutel. This appeared twice weekly, but then weekly several years later. In spring 1846, Dr. Albers, who had arrived from Cincinnati, started a second publication, the *Lokomotive*, which only lasted but a few months, as Albers joined a voluntary company, and served in the Mexican War at the rank of sergeant.

Later on, Albers returned to Cincinnati after the war, and edited the
Demokratisches Tageblatt, and then came into conflict with another newspaper editor
there, Emil Klauprecht. (7) In 1847, Walker tried his luck again in Louisville with a
publication called the *Patriot,* which, however, only lasted a few months. Another paper,
the *Louisville Bote,* was edited by a Mr. Rohrer and his family, which also printed and
delivered it. The *Beobachter* continued till 1855.

The Germans of Louisville belonged mainly to the Democratic Party. In the
presidential election of 1840, they had been mainly on this side of the fence, and
remained so in 1844. The problems, which took place in this year in Philadelphia as a
result of the nativists, who raged through the streets of town causing death and
destruction, had greatly upset all of the foreign-born, although the violence had been
directed apparently against the Irish Catholics. (8) The Democratic Party may have had a
number of ignorant, narrow-minded bigots in its ranks, but for the most part, its members
had campaigned for the rights of the adopted citizens and against the position of the
nativists.

Moreover, at the same time, the Whig Party of Kentucky was influenced by the
nativist spirit as well. George D. Prentice, who was as gifted and clever as also immoral
and devoid of character, edited the *Louisville Journal.* This was one of the most
influential Whig papers not only in Kentucky, but in the entire U.S. He had stoked the
fires of hate against the foreign-born by appealing to the lowest passions of the mob by
means of satire, and the lowest and most abusive kind of language. He referred to
immigrants as beggars, vagrants, scoundrels, and knaves.

It was, therefore, only natural that recent citizens would also become the targets
of such hostile attacks. Already before the elections, it came to hostilities, and resulted in
the Germans arming themselves for protection and then defeating and driving off those
who had attacked them. The publications of the nativists then attacked and accused them
of being atheists, who were disturbing the peace, and denounced them as conspirators

against the real and true children and rulers of the land. On election day, 4 August 1844, it came to a number of tumultuous events. Several German Democrats were driven away by ruffians stationed at voting places.

The editor of the *Beobachter* on learning of this issued a printed call to the Germans, warning them to arm themselves, and to respond to force in like manner. The *Journal* immediately had this translated and printed with the vilest commentary, and then distributed this throughout the city. A large mob gathered at the press of the *Beobachter*, and demanded to see the editors, who having caught wind of the approaching storm, had escaped to a safe location.

Dr. Holland, a gifted speaker, who had played an important role for a time as a Democratic Party speaker and writer in the western states, as well as Philipp Tomppert, who had succeeded in attracting quite a bit of Whig hostility in their speech-making during the electoral campaigns, were sought by the raging mob, but they had brought the saving Ohio River between them and their pursuers, and waited for several days in Indiana till calm had again returned. At several voting places, it came to bloody confrontations. (9)

Under the name of the National Guard, the Germans of Louisville had formed a militia company in 1846. Some of the most respected citizens of the city were members. It soon divided into two companies. In 1847, an artillery company was also formed, as well as an infantry company, which was named the U.S. Union Guard. In 1850, and later, German-American companies were formed. They took part in the 1846 Mexican War, and formed an infantry regiment, while some joined into the cavalry regiment formed by Kentucky.

Here was elsewhere, German-Americans were most interested in the events in the Fatherland. Immediately after the outbreak of the 1848 Revolution, a number of societies formed to support it, and in which, as we are told by Ludwig Stierlin, Dr. Caspari, an important personality considered one of the noblest and most gracious persons in

Louisville, played an important role. (10) These societies welcomed the refugees with open arms, as they streamed here after the failure of the revolution.

Louisville became for a time, one might say coincidentally, a gathering place for some of the brightest, and indeed one could even say, most interesting persons, which the waves of reaction in Europe had caused to land on American shores. However, the events of these highly interesting times and their associated aspirations do not belong to the time period we are concerned with here, but rather to the 1850s. (11)

The most remarkable event of the year 1848, according to Stierlin, was the founding of the German singing society, the Liederkranz, and is all that more noteworthy as it was not founded by the Forty-Eighters, but rather owes its founding to the date of the anniversary of the French Revolution, the mother of all revolutions, which took place on 12 February 1848. It is certainly a wonderful testimony to the citizens of Louisville at the time that they founded a society, which aimed to foster and unite its love of song with that of their love for the arts and education.

They, however, quickly realized that a society could not aspire to multiple goals at the same time, and, therefore, formed another society for the latter purposes, the Hermann-Verein, which later developed into a beneficial society. Also formed in the same year, was a *Freier Gesellschaftsbund*, which also had a choral section.

We might add that in the year 1848 only individual German refugees arrived here, of which several then returned in 1849. Also, in 1849, the number of arriving Forty-Eighters was still slight. Only in 1850 and 1851 did the numbers increase of those, who sought refuge here. They soon made their presence known by means of their various publications, as well as by their public speaking in the area. And, their influence, after the first illusions and immature communistic and socialistic fantasies had vanished, proved to be exceptionally fruitful, lively, and salutary. (12)

At the voting place, they really started to have an impact by the mid-1850s throughout the U.S., and the Republican victories, which were hotly contested with the help of the Germans in 1854-56, depended on the votes of the Germans, who had come earlier, and who found it difficult to switch parties from the Democrats under whose flag they had fought for years, to the Republicans, where they found their former enemies, the Whigs, as well as their most detested enemy, the Know-Nothings.

It was much easier for the recently arrived Forty-Eighters to join the newly formed Republican Party, which represented for them the ideals of the day and seemed to be more progressive.

In other cities of Kentucky, like Lexington, Maysville, Paducah, Germans could be found early on, but they did not exert the kind of influence as they did in Louisville. Newport and Covington, located directly across the Ohio River from Cincinnati, also had sizable and active German populations, but really formed an integral part of this area. (13)

Mention should also be made of the rural areas of Kentucky. In earlier times, Germans from the east had also settled in various parts of the state, while clearly avoiding the slave states of the South. (14)

Chapter Six

Indiana

Indiana – Early Lack of a Commercial Center – German Newspapers – Albert Lange – Johann B. Lutz (Mansfield – Wilhelm Heilmann – Bishop J.H. Luers – Johann Georg Rapp

Early on, Indiana lacked a center of business and industry that would have attracted the German immigration in great numbers. Along the Ohio River, there certainly are a number of well-situated and blossoming towns, such as Vevay, which introduced viticulture to Indiana; New Abany, located across from Louisville; Madison; and further on down the Ohio River Evansville. However, Cincinnati and Louisville were much further ahead of them and had already become centers of business and industry. The political capitol of the state, Indianapolis, had only 2,500 inhabitants in 1840 and although connected by canals with the Ohio and Wabash Rivers, only developed when it became a railway junction, and especially during and after the Civil War. (1)

From the 1830s on, many Germans had come to the state, especially to the northern part of the same, particularly to Fort Wayne, which later on became an important destination for Germans. By 1840, it possessed a Lutheran theological seminary, the Concordia College, which developed into a thriving institution. Germans also settled in the beautifully towns situated along the Wabash, including Vincennes, Terre Haute and Lafayette. However, nowhere could the German element really makes its presence known due to its geographical dispersion, even as it contributed everywhere to the growth and development of agriculture, business and industry, and the development of the arts.

Elsewhere we have discussed Johann Georg Rapp's colony of New Harmony elsewhere, but suffice it to say here that it undoubtedly left an enduring legacy, as it introduced an efficient system of agriculture and also contributed to pioneering industrial enterprises in Indiana. (Editor's Note: See the Supplement at the end of this chapter for Koerner's discussion of Rapp, which is from his chapter on Pennsylvania in *The German Element in the Northeast: Pennsylvania, New York, New Jersey and New England*)).

The first trace of a German newspaper we find in Indianapolis, where the wandering publisher Georg Walker brought out the *Hochwächter* for a time in 1845. In 1847, the weekly *Indiana Volksblatt* of Julius Bötticher appeared as well. Only by the 1850s, did the real era of the German element come about as a result of the substantial, and more well educated immigration that followed the 1848 Revolution. The growth and development of the German element proceeded rapidly, with Germans making a praiseworthy name in every branch of learning, industry, and politics. However, several individuals, who arrived before that date should be mentioned here as well.

Albert Lange was born almost at the same time as Francis Lieber, on 16 December 1801, in Charlottenburg near Berlin. He was the son of an outstanding physician and his only brother was an officer in the Prussian army. Like Lieber in Berlin, Lange in nearby Charlottenburg also detested the foreign rule of the French as a boy that oppressed Prussia and the despotic nature of this rule in particular. It is likely that during his years of study at the gymnasium in Berlin that he joined the large group of Turners under the direction of Jahn and others, which aimed to strengthen body and mind so as to prepare useful and patriotic citizens for the benefit of the fatherland. We know that he entered the University of Halle at age eighteen filled with notions of freedom and ideals, which enthused so much of the German youth, which had participated in the wars of liberation against Napoleon, or at least had lived through this time.

At the university Lange studied not only law, but also history and philosophy. He had become a member of the *Burschenschaft* there that was enthused with the idea of German freedom and unity, but at this time, had nothing more than certain revolutionary ideas in mind, but least of all was guilty of any treasonable conspiracies. A few of the most enthusiastic of its members may very well have made some impractical plans for small uprisings, but only the suspicions emanating from the ill will of the ruling regimes of the German states could find any treasonable conspirators among the members of the *Burschenschaft* during the years from 1817 to 1824. Nonetheless, many of the best members of the German youth fell victim to the reactionary persecutions of the German governments, especially that of Prussia.

We have often spoken of those who sought refuge in America, such as Fehrentheil, the Wesselhöfts, Karl Follen, Dr. Beck, Franz Lieber, etc. Lange also was also a victim of this terribly reactionary time. Locked up due to his involvement in various student activities, he was given a sentence of fifteen years, and sent to the Fortress Glogau to do his time. His first year was very hard, later some alleviation of this harshness was allowed. He was able to engage in intellectual activities and could take walks within the fortress. After five years, he was pardoned by means of a cabinet order of the king, and set free. While in prison, he had already resolved to immigrate to the U.S., and learned not only English, but also read works dealing with America. It is said that he seriously studied the U.S. Constitution, and read and translated the speeches of American statesmen. After his release, he remained for a short time in Germany, as this was had been allowed him, and in 1829, he arrived on American shores.

After a short stay in Cincinnati, he settled down in Hancock County, located ten miles west of Indianapolis, in order to engage in farming. Here he met and married the daughter of an old settler. We do not know if farming appealed to him or not, only that in 1836 he moved to the nicely situated town of Terre Haute, located along the Wabash River, which with various short interruptions, became his permanent place of residence. He was elected justice of the peace, a position he held for many years, and distinguished himself by his thorough knowledge of the law and the conscientious execution of his position.

From the very first, Lange participated actively in politics, and belonged to the Whig Party, which was an exception among Germans. He became a recognized leader of his party, and was valued all that much more by the Whigs, since he was German, and could exert influence on his countrymen, who mainly then belonged to the Democratic

Party, and they hope to make good use of him. Henry Clay was for him the foremost statesman of the country. It was therefore natural that when the Whigs won the election of 1849 with General Taylor and Millard Fillmore that Lange was awarded with an appointment as U.S. consul to Amsterdam. To rise from the status of an exile from Europe to such a highly regarded position was something that brought Lange a great deal of personal satisfaction. This office itself, however, was not financially rewarding, thus causing him to resign from it after a short time, and he then accepted a position with the Department of the Interior. He returned to Terre Haute, and was soon elected as County Auditor, a position he held for eight years. Although he always thought and spoke decisively on political questions, he was nonetheless just as likable and honorable a person as he was generally popular, not only in his own county, but across the state.

Like many others in the Whig Party, he joined the newly formed Republican Party in 1856, and was elected to the position of state auditor in 1860 on the Republican ticket. This made a move to Indianapolis, the capital of the state, necessary. The Civil War made his position a very difficult one, as the task at hand was to respond to the call of the President to provide the necessary forces for the war, including the recruitment, care, and arming of the troops before they entered the service of the U.S. Army. The very energetic Governor Morton was actively supported by a circle of higher officials in state government, which essentially formed his cabinet, and succeeded not only in meeting the first quota of 5,000 men, but also in the course of summer 1861 of providing 40,000 more men. Lange distinguished himself especially by his enthusiasm and energy.

At the end of his term (1863), he returned to Terre Haute, where he was repeatedly elected as mayor. In the last years of his life, he focused on his law practice, especially the investigation of property titles. After a short illness, he died on 25 July 1869. His passing was deeply mourned, and his funeral was one of the most magnificent that Terre Haute had ever had. The Governor and other high officials from the state capitol were in attendance. The mayor, city council, and all public officials of the town and the county attended his funeral, as did members of the German singing societies and the Turners. R. W. Thompson, one of the most respected and eloquent men and speakers of Indiana, now (1879) Secretary of the Navy, who belonged with Lange to a Masonic lodge, spoke at the funeral. One of the resolutions passed in his honor came from the city council and describes Lange's character so perfectly that he can only adopt it as being totally in accord with our view of him. The resolution states as follows:

Lange was an exceptional human being. He was very well educated, noble, and just. In political life he enjoyed great influence, and did honor to the positions that he held. In public life he distinguished himself by means of his sociability and urbanity, was charitable and supported the poor and unfortunate.

Johann B. Lutz (Mansfield) was born in the first years of the nineteenth century, probably in Braunschweig or Hannover, and enjoyed a classical education at the University of Göttingen. Involvement in the student unrest caused him to flee from Germany, and immigrate to the U.S. In the early 1830s, we find him as professor mathematics at the Transylvania University in Lexington, Kentucky. He was, as Jahn used to say of the Lützower Friesen who had fallen in the field in France, "a highly gifted and blessed Siegfried figure." Over six feet tall, he was slender and very muscular. Rich brown locks covered his head. His face was of real beauty, his eyes large and dark blue. No river was too wide for him from to swim across. He also was an excellent Turner, swordsman, and skilled marksman, as well as an energetic dancer. At the latter he was considered a good teacher, was personable, and quite popular with the ladies in the aristocratic circles of Lexington.

Lutz lived there a number of years, and married an American lady in the 1840s, who apparently married under the condition he take on her family's surname. When he left Kentucky in 1850 for Madison, Indiana, located along the Ohio River, he bore this name. In the vicinity of Madison, living in very nice circumstances, he built a beautiful country home, which stopping place for many interesting and well educated men and women, as well as a point of attraction for social life in and around Madison. He actively took part in politics and was, if we are not mistaken, one of the delegates of Indiana at the

Republican convention in Chicago (1860) that nominated Lincoln as a presidential candidate.

During the Civil War, he was appointed commandant of the entire militia of Indiana with the rank of Major General at the time of the raid of the Confederates under General Morgan. Later, he held a military position that required him to move to Indianapolis. After war's end, in 1865, he sold his land along the Ohio River, and moved his family to Indianapolis, where he lived in retirement. In 1870, when Illinois established a new railway from Bloomington to Danville, Mansfield bought land in Piatt County and laid out the town, which was named Mansfield after him. Here he had a home built and lived with his family till his death on 20 September 1876.

Still at the height of his strength, we find a man, at whose birth no one could have prophesied his future. We refer here to Wilhelm Heilmann, who was born on 11 October 1824 in Albig in the Grand Duchy of Hessen-Darmstadt. He had the misfortune of loosing his father, a farmer, during his youth. Nevertheless, he received a good school education and worked with his step-father, Peter Weintz, who was also a farmer. Heilmann immigrated to America in 1843, bought a farm in Posey County, Indiana, and engaged in farming there. However, he soon sought a more rewarding occupation. Provided with a small amount of funds, he joined his brother-in-law, an experienced machinist, in opening a business for the production of machinery in Evansville. In log workshop they began their iron foundry. As we learn from a speech of Heilmann's, presented in Congress on 9 May 1879, the business grew greatly from these humble beginnings.

In this speech Heilmann spoke against the increased use of paper money and against the payment of our debts with bad money, or money that was not actually real. And, since he was the kind of a person, who believes that the shortest distance between two points is a straight line, he maintained that "honesty lasts the longest," and that people like him were usually referred to as wealthy capitalists, so that he would like to take the took the opportunity of saying a few words about himself. "I definitely am not a capitalist full of government loans. I have no such loans. I am a simple manufacturer and speak in the interest of those that work. I came to this country at age nineteen with out a dollar in my pocket. After working hard, I saved five hundred dollars from my earnings. The driving force of the factory was a blind work-horse. That kind of work is on target in this country that forms capital. In the beginning, the factory only employed six workers, but the quality of the work and the honesty of the business led to a greater clientele. In 1850, a brick building was built and a steam engine replaced the horse."

Heilmann distinguished himself as an extremely shrewd and calculating businessman. He established business connections everywhere, as his foundry expanded from year to year, and instead of a small log building his factory now consists of gigantic buildings that take up almost an area the size of a residential section of this beautiful town. The foundry is one of the largest in the West and employs two hundred workers. In the middle of a beautiful park, Heilmann built one of the most elegant homes in the state of Indiana. However, his own business, as large as it is, did not hinder him from taking part in contributions to the well-being and flourishing of his hometown. He participated in all ventures aimed in that direction, serving mostly in the office as president or as a director. He is president of the gas, the streetcar, and cotton manufacturing companies, director of the Evansville National Bank, as well as several other railways that pass through Evansville.

Heilmann did not take part in politics earlier in his life, but belonged to the Republican Party and did much to support it. During the Civil War, he demonstrated the strongest support for the Union at every opportunity and generously gave to all the collections for patriotic purposes, which those not in the military service usually get organized. He was a member of the city council on numerous occasions from 1852 onwards. But only after the war was he encouraged to actively campaign for other political offices. In 1870, he was elected to the state legislature, and in 1872, the Republicans nominated him as candidate for Congress, but even though he did better than other candidates of his party, they were all overcome by the Democratic majority. In 1876, he was elected to the state senate, and in 1878, he succeeded in getting elected to the Congress. A strong, well-built and muscular man of great stature with a broad full forehead, he is a man of action and creativity whose in-born good sense took the place of a scholarly and theoretical education. He is not an eloquent speaker, but his clear and natural way of expressing himself gets him the attention and approval of his listeners. Here we can best call upon him to prove this. In the aforementioned speech, he said the following after making his introduction:

> I do not boast about being talented in public speaking. Almost my entire life was devoted to business activities and partly because of this as a businessman I was afforded the honor by the people of the first district of Indiana of representing them in Congress after this district has been Democratic for many years. The people feel, as I do, that the world is governed too much and that the creation of legislative proposals by the thousands and the flooding of the country with laws, resolutions and amendments is something that should be brought to a halt for a while.

> This lawmaking activity really is not that astonishing on the whole, when one considers that approximately five-sixths of the members of Congress are lawyers, who take such great pleasure at lawmaking, just as much as others do at making money.

Heilmann's life story is emblematic of his hometown and the state of Indiana itself, with whose interests he is so closely connected. Just as one of the most flourishing states of the Union blossomed from a thinly settled state, viewed as one of the step-children of the western states, and which was regarded as left behind and without promise by others, so too did our farmer's son from Albig became a man second to none in terms of the practical value and influence he has had for the state as an honorable and intelligent man of great wealth.

In 1858, when Fort Wayne was elevated to rank of a Catholic bishopric, a German was sent to this sparsely settled region, Johann Heinrich Luers. He was born in 1819 near

Vechta in Oldenburg, and came to America with his parents. He studied at the seminary in Cincinnati and became a priest at the newly founded St. Joseph's Church in Cincinnati in 1846, where he quite effectively worked for the preservation of the German heritage. When he was entrusted with the episcopate of Fort Wayne twelve years later, he was at first irresolute if he should accept this appointment, or not. Luers was an enthusiastic student in the field of church history, possessed a rich library, including several incunabula, and had a deep appreciation for the German language and heritage. He died while on a professional trip to Cleveland, 28 June 1871.

Supplement

This Supplement is from: Gustav Koerner, *The German Element in the Northeast: Pennsylvania, New York, New Jersey, and New England.* Translated and edited by Don Heinrich Tolzmann (2010). It is from is from a chapter on Pennsylvania, where he discusses Rapp in greater detail than he does in his chapter on Indiana. (2)

**

Johann Georg Rapp

In a country that offered so much seemingly endless room for agriculture and was still relatively unpopulated, one can readily understand that farming was not that advanced. The land was exploited with the certainty that one could always find fresh land at a cheap price in the West. It was not unusual for one to farm for only what needed for one's own family. One's other time was spent hunting, fishing and in other kinds of activities. The immigrants of earlier times probably had not established a true sense of homeland as yet, at least not strong enough to bind them to the place they first settled, especially if they thought there were more favorable prospects elsewhere.

The stronger orientation of the Germans, on the other hand, and the tendency to hang on to their home place, which is a trait unique to Germans, was actually the reason that caused them to establish a firm and lasting home in not only in New York, New Jersey, but especially in Pennsylvania. They engaged in more rational kinds of farming and constructed more substantial barns and granaries than their American, especially Scotch-Irish neighbors.

Their example was imitated and there is no doubt that since the earliest times, German farmers have contributed to the advancement of agriculture in this country. In the area of farming and small industry there probably is hardly a German settlement that has accomplished more and provided a better example for others than the one established in

Pennsylvania by Johann Georg Rapp, a weaver and farmer. (3) He was born in 1770 in Maulbronn in Württemberg (some sources indicate 1757 as the year of his birth), but as the last twenty-seven years of Rapp's life fall within the time period of this work, we shall taken him into consideration here.

As a result of dissatisfaction with the religious orthodoxy of his time, Rapp came to reject all religious ceremonies and sacraments. He aimed to establish a community in accordance with his conception of the church of the first Christians. In his view, the only true way to salvation was by means of a direct relationship with God through Jesus Christ. He told the Prince Bernhard of Sachsen-Weimar, who visited him in New Harmony, which was the second settlement that he established in Indiana, that: "According to the teachings of Christ we must view ourselves as an individual family, where all work to the best of their strengths and abilities for the common good of all." (4)

His settlements, however, showed how impractical and unworkable his entire plan for a community was: he never allowed his community to grow (it never surpassed more than 800 members), he forbade marriage, and expelled all those considered idle, disobedient or unfit. Such individuals received a settlement for money they had donated, or earned for work they had done. His ideas, when applied to a nation, become immediately untenable: Imagine a state with one individual, even if an enlightened prophet, who is empowered with the right of dividing people into groups, can assign their work, and then expels those considered undesirable! His concept of a community was only possible within the framework of a large state that offered the possibility of refuge for those who had left his community.

After Rapp and several friends purchased land in Pennsylvania in 1803 (6,000 acres), mostly woodland in the vicinity of Pittsburgh, he then brought over about three hundred members of his group to their new home in the following year. (5) These hardworking farmers transformed the wilderness into a prosperous settlement under the greatest of hardships. It consisted of the town of Harmony and several smaller villages. They planted vineyards, cultivated fruit and raised livestock, especially sheep, developed machinery, and established weaving mills, dye-works, distilleries and other mills. They had stores with managers, enjoyed the greatest credit rating, as well as a reputation as a sound business enterprise, according to Franz von Lőher. What motivated Rapp to sell this beautiful settlement for a pittance in1813 and move west to Indiana remains a mystery. Perhaps it was the result of a vision of his.

The land in Indiana (30,000 acres of woodland) was in a fertile region where corn thrived, but due to its location in the lowlands near the Wabash River was endangered by frequent flooding, and so was not considered the best of locations. (6)Apparently, Rapp had the idea of establishing a cotton plantation there, but did not consider that Indiana was in a free state, and that this kind of agriculture was not carried on very well by whites. Fortunately, he succeeded in selling New Harmony to another well known visionary, Dale Robert Owen, who definitely was not as methodical as Rapp, our sturdy Swabian farmer. He was greatly supported in all his undertakings by his son, Friedrich Rapp, who was a better administrator and also had a knack for working well together with Americans, so much so that he attained and held high offices in Indiana.

Rapp then moved back to Pennsylvania in 1825 to establish a new settlement known as Economy, located near the Ohio River. In a splendid location on a knoll, he created a veritable paradise that became an exemplary business enterprise. All work was done by means of the best machinery, and in addition to the aforementioned industries, cotton and silk weaving was also begun. How wealthy this smaller colony actually was at the time of Rapp's death (1847) can only be estimated. Some estimates runs as high as $20,000,000, but I am doubtful of this figure, and consider it an overestimation.

Rapp was generally not well regarded by Germans, who viewed him negatively, not only as clever, but also as a deceptive. However, there was no basis for such opions. And, all those who visited him and saw him at work, had only the highest regard for him. This included a variety of well known travelers, including the American scholar Schoolcraft, the Scottish traveler Melish, the Englishman Cumming, as well as the Prince of Weimar, the latter of whom was repelled by Rapp's religious views and approached Rapp with a good bit of apprehension. (7)

Rapp might best be compared to another highly successful German immigrant: John Jacob Astor. (8) Both were farm boys, born not far from one another, who became well known for their hard work and have earned our respect. Talent and genius are but accidental gifts, but as Lessing comments: "Diligence is the only human attribute that one can truly celebrate." And it is exactly this untiring diligence, which demands not only daily, but hourly sacrifice in the battle against the inborn human inclination to laziness. In the case of Astor and Rapp, it was their enduring diligence that assured them the greatest possible success, and also contributed to their attaining great honor for the German name in this country.

Chapter Seven

Editor's Conclusion

Gustav Koerner provides us with a detailed portrait of the German element in the Ohio Valley by means of his biographical approach to writing history. It, therefore, certainly is the appropriate point of departure for anyone interested in exploring German influences and contributions to this area. Certainly many of the persons and topics he covers are worthy of further exploration and examination, and hopefully this work will contribute to further research and study.

Size of the Population (1870)

Although Koerner does make occasional use of statistics, he does not do so systematically. Statistical information is, therefore, provided here, to ascertain the size of the populations we are dealing with in each state covered here. A good source of such data is Alexander Schem's *Deutsch-Amerikanisches Konversations-Lexikon*, a German-American encyclopedia that was published after the Civil War, and contains data drawn from the U.S. Census (1870). This does yield information as to the size of the foreign-born populations, but not the American-born generations, so it does not give statistics as to the entirety of the size of the German element, but at least, provides us with data regarding the immigrant population per state.(1)

Ohio

Total Population: 2,665,260

German-born: 182,897

Swiss-born: 12,727

Austrian-born: 3,699

Population centers by county (top five)

- Hamilton: 55,273 German-born and 1,300 Swiss-born
- Cuyahoga: 19,334 German born and 916 Swiss-born

- Montgomery: 7,386 German-born and 159 Swiss-born
- Lucas: 6,804 German-born and 282 Swiss-born
- Franklin: 5,705 German-born and 282 Swiss-born

Kentucky

Total Population: 1,321,011

German-born: 36,319

Swiss-born: 1,147

Austrian-born: no data

Population centers by county (top five)

- Jefferson: 15,766 German-born and 697 Swiss-born
- Kenton: 4,880 German-born and 68 Swiss-born
- Campbell: 4,356 German-born and 106 Swiss-born
- McLean: 485 German-born and 23 Swiss-born
- Bracken: 377 German-born and 7 Swiss-born

Indiana

Total Population: 1,680,637

German-born: 123,060

Swiss-born: 4,285

Austrian-born: no data

Population centers by county (top five)

- Vanderburgh: 7,297 German-born and 157 Swiss-born
- Marion: 6,536 German-born and 243 Swiss-born
- Allen: 5,347 German-born and 311 Swiss-born
- LaPorte: 4,274 German-born and 78 Swiss-born
- Dearborn: 3,188 German-born and 35 Swiss-born

Civil War Service

Another topic that Koerner does not cover systematically is the Civil War service of German-Americans, and this is due to the fact that his primary focus is on the first half of the nineteenth century. Nevertheless, he does make occasional reference to this topic. Information regarding this topic is, therefore, provided here. Shirley J. Riemer's *The German Research Companion* provides the following information as to German units in the Civil War. (2)

Ohio

Infantry:

9th Ohio Regiment, 1st German regiment, from Cincinnati

28th Ohio Regiment, 2nd German regiment, from Cincinnati

37th Ohio Regiment, 3rd German regiment, from northern Ohio

47th Ohio Regiment (over half German)

58th Ohio Regiment (over half German)

74th Ohio Regiment (over half German)

106th Ohio Regiment, 4th German regiment

107th Ohio Regiment, 5th German regiment

108th Ohio Regiment, 6th German regiment

165th and 65th Ohio Regiment (over half German)

Cavalry:

3rd Ohio Cavalry (partly German)

Artillery:

Dilger's Battery, Battery I, 1st Light Artillery, originally von Dammert's battery from Cincinnati

Hofman's Battery, 4th Ohio Battery, from Cincinnati

Markgraf's Battery, 8th Independent Battery, from Cincinnati (half German)

20th Ohio Independent Battery, from Cleveland (about half German)

Indiana

Infantry:

14th Indiana Regiment (half German; Company E all German)

24th Indiana Regiment (half German)

32nd Indiana Regiment, from southeast Indiana

136th Indiana Regiment, from Evansville (half German)

Artillery:

Behr's Battery, 6th Independent Indiana Battery, from Indianapolis

Klaus's Battery, 1st Independent Indiana Battery, from Evansville

Kentucky

Infantry:

5th Kentucky Regiment, from Louisville (half German)

6th Kentucky Regiment, from Louisville (half German)

Cavalry:

2nd Kentucky Cavalry (had many Germans)

Artillery:

Stone's Battery, Battery A, 1st Regiment Light Artillery, independent (had many Germans)

A Basic Source

In the tri-state region of Ohio, Kentucky, and Indiana the total population (1870) numbered 5,666,848, of which the German, Swiss, and Austrian-born populations amounted to a total of 364,134. Although it is impossible to estimate the total size of the German element that would include the American-born descendants, the number would no doubt be considerable. The impact of the German immigration on Ohio, Kentucky, and Indiana is clearly evidenced nonetheless by this statistical enumeration, as is the substantial number of German units formed for the Union cause during the Civil War: 16 infantry regiments, 6 artillery units, and 2 cavalry units. These contributions in addition to those discussed by Koerner clearly demonstrate how important it is to take German immigration and settlement into consideration when it comes to a history of the states of the Ohio Valley under consideration here.

Since the publication of Koerner's history in 1880, German immigration has, of course, continued on up to the present time, thereby contributing to the growth of the population of German ancestry. The German element experienced some tumultuous times in the first half of the 20th century with the advent of two world wars against the ancestral homeland, which brought with them a tragic display of anti-German hysteria and sentiment. However, the second half of the 20th century brought with it many positive events that have contributed to renewed interest in German heritage and culture throughout the U.S. This included the celebration of the German-American Tricentennial in 1983, the establishment of German-American Day in 1987, and the unification of Germany in 1990. The story of these intervening years since the late nineteenth century is properly the topic for another work dealing with the German element in the states covered by this volume, but one which of necessity would have to take a look at Koerner's work as one of the basic sources for the foundational years of that history. (3)

Sources

The sources Koerner used for his German-American history were predominantly in the German language. A copy of them follows for those interested in further research with these source materials. References to more recent sources are provided in the notes for this edition. For further references to primary and secondary sources, see the following bibliographies by the editor of this volume: *German-Americana: A Bibliography*. (Metuchen, New Jersey: Scarecrow Press, 1975), and also by the same author: *Catalog of the German-Americana Collection, University of Cincinnati*. (München: K.G. Saur, 1990). And, for a general history of the German element in America, see the author's: *The German-American Experience*. A Revised and Expanded Edition of Theodore Huebener's The Germans in America. (Amherst, New York: Humanity Books, 2000).

Quellen.

Eine sehr ausgedehnte Korrespondenz, sowohl mit vielen der Männer, die in diesem Buche erwähnt werden, als auch mit Literaten und Redakteuren deutscher Zeitungen in den Vereinigten Staaten, hat uns die werthvollsten Mittheilungen gebracht und uns, nebst eigenen Ergänzungen, das größte Material geliefert. Die nachstehenden Schriften sind außerdem die vorzüglichsten, welche wir benutzt haben:

1. CHARLES FOLLEN'S WORKS, edited by his widow E. C. FOLLEN, 3 vol., Boston, 1846.
2. Life of CHARLES FOLLEN. By same.
3. Franz Löher. „Geschichte und Zustände der Deutschen in Amerika". Cincinnati, Eggers und Wulkop, 1847; Leipzig, bei K. F. Köhler.
4. Friedrich Kapp. „Geschichte der deutschen Einwanderung im Staate New York, bis zum Anfang des 19. Jahrhunderts". 3. Auflage. New York, E. Steiger.
5. Friedrich Münch. „Erinnerungen aus Deutschland's trübster Zeit". St. Louis und Neustadt a. d. Hardt, Konrad Witter.
6. Reise Sr. Hoheit des Herzogs Bernhard zu Sachsen-Weimar-Eisenach durch Nord Amerika in den Jahren 1825 und 1826. Herausgegeben von Heinrich Luden. 2 Theile. Weimar, Wilhelm Hoffmann, 1828.
7. W. O. von Horn. „Johann Jakob Astor". New York, E. Steiger, 1868.
8. Ferdinand Ernst. „Bemerkungen auf einer Reise durch das Innere der vereinigten Staaten von Nordamerika im Jahre 1819". Hildesheim bei Gerstenberg, 1820.
9. Reisebericht der Familien Köpfli und Suppiger aus Neu-Schweizerland, Illinois. Sursee, 1833.
10. Theodor E. Hilgard. „Erinnerungen". Als Manuskript gedruckt. Heidelberg.
11. „Anzeiger des Westens". St. Louis. Jahrgänge 1835—1850.
12. „Belleville Beobachter". Belleville, 1844.
13. „Belleviller Zeitung". Belleville, Jahrgang 1849.
14. „Alte und Neue Welt". Philadelphia, Jahrgänge 1834—1844.
15. „Cincinnati Volksblatt". Jahrgänge 1836—1850.
16. „Der Hochwächter". (Georg Walker.) Cincinnati, Jahrgänge 1845—49.
17. „Der Deutsche Pionier". Monatsschrift des deutschen Pionierlebens in Amerika. Cincinnati, Jahrgänge 1—11 (1869—1879).
18. Life and Letters of Washington Irving, 4 volumes. New York, Putnam and Co.

(433)

434   Das deutsche Element in den Ver. Staaten 1818—1848.

19. WASHINGTON IRVING. "Astoria". Philadelphia, Carey, Lee and Blanchard, 1826.
20. Gert Göbel. „Länger als ein Menschenleben in Missouri". St. Louis, Konrad Witter, 1877.
21. PIERCE. "Charles Sumner's Memoirs and Letters". Boston, 1877.
22. FRANCIS LIEBER. "Political Ethics".
23. FRANCIS LIEBER. "Letters to a Gentleman in Germany". Philadelphia, 1834.
24. Franz Lieber. „Tagebuch meines Aufenthalt's in Griechenland". Leipzig, bei Brockhaus, 1823.
25. Life, Character and Writings of Francis Lieber. A discourse delivered before the Historical Society of Pennsylvania, by M. Russel Thayer. Philadelphia, 1873.
26. Lieber's Writings and Pamphlets.
27. Dr. Oswald Seidensticker. „Geschichte der „Deutschen Gesellschaft" von Pennsylvanien von 1764—1876". Philadelphia, Jgnatz Kohler und Schäfer und Korabi, 1876.
28. J. G. Wesselhöft. „Selbstbiographie". Manuskript.
29. FRANCIS S. DRAKE. "Dictionary of American Biography". Boston, Osgood and Co., 1872.
30. E. A. and GEO. L. DUYCKINCK. "Cyclopædia of American Literature". New York, Chas. Scribner, 1856.
31. Dr. J. G. Büttner. „Die Vereinigten Staaten von Nord Amerika". 2 Bände. Hamburg, 1844.
32. Dr. J. G. Büttner. „Briefe aus und über die Vereinigten Staaten". 2 Bände. Dresden, 1846.
33. Emil Klauprecht. „Deutsche Chronik in der Geschichte des Ohiothales". Cincinnati, Hof und Jakobi, 1864.
34. „Das Westland". Nordamerikanische Zeitschrift für Deutschland von Dr. G. Engelmann und Karl Neyfeld. Heidelberg, bei Engelmann, 1837—1838.
35. Alexander Schem. „Deutsch-amerikanisches Konversations-Lexicon". 11 Bände, New York, 1869—1874.
36. CHARLES NORDHOFF. "The Cotton States." New York, Scribner, 1876.
37. CHARLES NORDHOFF's Works, generally.
38. Rudolph A. Koß. „Milwaukee." Milwaukee, Verlag des „Herold", 1872.
39. Armin Tenner. „Cincinnati Sonst und Jetzt". Cincinnati, Mecklenborg und Rosenthal, 1878.
40. M. JOBLIN AND JAMES LANDY. "Cincinnati Past and Present". Cincinnati, 1872.
41. The Biographical Encyclopædia of Ohio of the 19. Century. Cincinnati and Philadelphia, Galaxy Publishing Company, 1876.
42. American Biographical Dictionary for Illinois. New York, 1873.
43. WM. H. EGLE. "History of the Commonwealth of Pennsylvania". Harrisburg, 1877.
44. WHITELAW REID. "Ohio in the War". 2. Vol., Cincinnati, 1868.
45. „Der deutsche Kirchenfreund". Redigirt von Dr. Ph. Schaff. Mercersburg, Pennsylvanien, 1848—1850.

Quellen.   435

46. Wm. B. Sprague. "Annals of the American Lutheran Pulpit".
    New-York, 1869.
47. L. Stierlin. „Der Staat Kentucky und die Stadt Louisville". 1873.
48. Ferdinand Römer. „Texas". Bonn, 1849.
49. Hermann Ehrenberg. „Texas und die Revolution." Leipzig, 1843.
50. Reports of the Santa Rita Silver Mining Company. Cincinnati, 1859
    —1860.
51. Reports of the Sonora Exploring and Mining Company. Cincinnati,
    1856, 1858—1860.
52. Dr. Th. Logan. "Memoir of the Life and Services of Dr. C. A.
    Luetzenburg". New Orleans, 1848.
53. H. A. Rattermann. „General Johann Andreas Wagener. Eine biographi-
    sche Skizze". Cincinnati, 1877.
54. Schriftliche Notizen über Ferd. Rud. Haßler, von seinen Töchtern.
55. Emil Zschokke. „Ingenieur F. R. Haßler." Aarau, Sauerländer 1877.

Notes

Preface

1. See; Gustav Koerner, *Das deutsche Element in den Vereinigten Staaten von Nordamerika, 1818-1848*. (Cincinnati: A.E. Wilde & Co., 1880).

2. See the following works I have edited: *Illinois' German Heritage*. (Milford, Ohio: Little Miami Pub. Co., 2005); *Missouri's German Heritage*. 2nd edition. (Milford, Ohio: Little Miami Pub. Co., 2006); and: Gustav Koerner, *The German Element in the Northeast: Pennsylvania, New York, New Jersey, and New England*. (Baltimore, Maryland: Clearfield Co., 2010).

Editor's Introduction

1. For further information on Koerner, see: Evarts B. Greene, "Gustave Koerner," in: Tolzmann, ed., *Illinois' German Heritage*, pp. 93-103.

2. Regarding the *Burschenschaft*, see: Tolzmann, ed., *Missouri's German Heriatge*, pp. 1. For further information about the uprising of 1832-33 in Germany, see: Joachim Kermann, Gehard Nestler and Dieter Schiffmann, eds., *Freiheit, Einheit und Europa: Das Hambacher Fest von 1832 – Ursachen, Ziele und Wirkungen*. (Ludwighafen: Verlag Pro Message, 2006).

3. Regarding Koerner's involvement in the Frankfurt Uprising, see: Greene, "Gustave Koerner," p. 96.

4. For a discussion of Duden and the importance of his book about America, see: Dorris Keeven-Franke, "Gottfried Duden: The Man behind the Book," in: Tolzmann, ed., *Missouri's German Heritage*, pp. 85-95.

5. For Koerner's history of Belleville and southern Illinois, see: Gustav Koerner, "Southern Illinois," in: Tolzmann, ed., *Illinois' German Heritage*, pp. 5-42.

6. See: Koerner, *Das deutsche Element*, p. 6.

7. For references to Koerner's correspondence with Lincoln, see: Tolzmann, ed., *Illinois' German Heritage*, p. 105.

8. For Koerner's autobiography, see Gustav Koerner, *Memoirs of Gustave Koerner, 1809-1896: Life Sketches Written at the Suggestion of His Children*. 2 vols. Edited by Thomas J. McCormack. (Cedar Rapids, Iowa: The Torch Press, 1909).

9. See: Julius Goebel, "Gustav Koerner," *Dictionary of American Biography*.

10. See: Koerner, *Das deutsche Element*, pp. 5-18.

11. Ibid, 6.

12. Ibid.

13. Ibid.

14. Ibid, p. 7.

15. Ibid, p. 9. The reference to Franz von Löher is to his German-American history entitled: : *Geschichte und Zustände der Deutschen in Amerika*. (Cincinnati: Verlag von Eggers und Wulkop, 1847).

16. Ibid, pp. 11-12.

17. Ibid, p. 11.

18. Ibid, pp. 20-21.

19. Ibid, p. 8.

20. Ibid, pp. 16-17.

21. Ibid.

22. See: Koerner, *Das Deutsche Element*, pp. 177—244, 351-56.

Chapter 1

1. Joseph Michael Bäumler (?-1853) led a group of about three hundred Swabian immigrants to Ohio in 1817, and established a community in Tuscarawas County. In 1819, they founded the Zoar Society of Separatists, and the settlement became known as Zoar. See: Don Heinrich Tolzmann, *German Heritage Guide to the State of Ohio*. (Milford, Ohio: Little Miami Pub. Co., 2005), p. 7. The reference to German separatists in Pennsylvania relates to the settlement established there by Johann Georg Rapp. For further information about him, see Chapter 6, which discusses his settlement there, as well as in Indiana.

2. For the standard history of Zoar, see: Emilius O. Randall, *History of the Zoar Society, from its Commencement to its Conclusion: A Sociological Study in Communism.* 3rd. ed. (Columbus, Ohio: F.J. Heer, 1904).

3. For further information on Ziegler and Baum, see: Max Burgheim, *Cincinnati in Wort und Bild. Mit zahlreichen Illustrationen.* (Cincinnati, Ohio: Burgheim Publishing Co., 1891), pp. 41-43, 51; Don Heinrich Tolzmann, *The German Heritage Guide to the Greater Cincinnati Area.* 2nd ed. (Milford, Ohio: Little Miami Pub. Co., 2007), pp. 47-48; and: Henry Howe, *Hamilton County, Ohio: As Extracted from Henry Howe's Historical Collections of Ohio.* Edited by Barbara Keyser Garguilo. (Milford, Ohio: Little Miami Pub. Co., 2005), pp. 115, 121-23.

4. See: Emil Klauprecht, *German Chronicle in the History of the Ohio Valley, and its Capital City Cincinnati, in Particular.* Translated by Dale Lally, Jr. and edited by Don Heinrich Tolzmann. (Bowie, Maryland: Heritage Books, Inc., 1992), p. 156.

5. Regarding Burkhalter, see: Klauprecht, *German Chronicle*, pp. 156, 177; Burgheim,; Burgheim, *Cincinnati*, p. 70; Tolzmann, *German Heritage Guide to the Greater Cincinnati Area*, p. 10; and: Howe, *Hamilton County*, p. 115-16.

6. For further information on Stein, see: Klauprecht, *German Chronicle*, p. 166; Burgheim, *Cincinnati*, p. 70; Tolzmann, *German Heritage Guide to the Queen City*, p. 77; Howe, *Hamilton County*, p. 117.

7. For the early history of German religious life in Cincinnati, see: Don Heinrich Tolzmann, *Cincinnati's German Heritage.* (Bowie, Maryland: Heritage Books, Inc., 1994), Part I, pp. 52-69, and also: Klauprecht, *German Chronicle*, pp. 171-80.

8. Regarding Reese, see: Klauprecht, *German Chronicle*, pp. 157, 160, 173, and Tolzmann, *German Heritage Guide to the Greater Cincinnati Area*, p. 76. Also, see: Don Heinrich Tolzmann, ed., *Das Ohiotal – the Ohio Valley: The German Dimension.* (New York: Peter Lang Pub. Co., 1993), pp. 28.

9. For the early history of the German press of Cincinnati, see: Klauprecht, *German Chronicle*, especially Chapter 28, and: Burgheim, *Cincinnati*, pp. 118-45.

10. For a biography of Nast, see: Carl Wittke, *William Nast, Patriarch of German Methodism.* (Detroit: Wayne State University Press, 1959), and: Howe, *Hamilton County*, p. 116.

11. Regarding these newspapers, see: Klauprecht, *German Chronicle*, especially Chapter 28, and also, see footnote no. 9.

12. Ibid.

13. For Weber's survey of the German-American press, see: Wilhelm Weber, "Die Zeitungen in den Vereinigten Staaten; mit besonderer Berücksichtigung der in deutscher Sprache erscheinenden Blätter," in: Karl J.R. Arndt and May E. Olson, eds., *The German Language Press of the Americas: Volume 3: German-American Press Research from the American Revolution to the Bicentennial.* (München: K.G. Saur, 1980), pp. 473-513.

14. Koerner does not indicate where Kapp's article appeared, but it was most likely in one of the German-American newspapers of New York, such as the *New Yorker Staats-Zeitung*. Friedrich Kapp (1824-84) was a Forty-Eighter, who lived in America from 1850-70, editing German-American newspapers and writing several German-American historical works, but then returned to Germany, where he served in the Reichstag. For biographical information, see: Horst Dippel, "Kapp, Friedrich," in: *Neue Deutsche Biographie*, Vol. 11, pp. 134ff. Also, see: H.A. Rattermann, "Friedrich Kapp," *Deutsch-Amerikanisches Magazin.* 1(1887): 16-36, 226-238, and 360-373. Rattermann also provides a bibliography of Kapp's publications, pp. 371-73.

15. See footnote no. 13.

16. For a history of the German Society of New York, see: Klaus Wust, *Guardian on the Hudson: The German Society of the City of New York, 1784-1984.* (New York: German Society of the City of New York, 1984).

17. Regarding the formation of Cincinnati's first German society, see: Tolzmann, *Cincinnati's German Heritage*, Part I, pp. 69-70.

18. For information on these militia organizations, see: Tolzmann, *German Heritage Guide to the Greater Cincinnati Area*, p. 15.

19. For further information about Stallo, see: Klauprecht, *German Chronicle*, pp. 182, 185, 195-96; Burgheim, *Cincinnati*, p. 87; Tolzmann, *German Heritage Guide to the Greater Cincinnati Area*, pp. 18, 77; and: Howe, *Hamilton County*, p. 116.

20. Regarding Rümelin, see: Klauprecht, *German Chronicle*, pp. 171-72, 178, and 183, and: Burgheim, *Cincinnati*, p. 87.

21. Regarding Gottfried Duden and the importance of his book for the history of the German immigration, see: Tolzmann, ed., *Das Ohiotal*, pp. 28-31.

22. Regarding German-American support of the Republican Party, see: Tolzmann, *German Heritage Guide to the Greater Cincinnati Area*, pp. 17-18.

23. This most likely from his autobiography: *Life of Charles Reemelin, German: Carl Gustav Rümelin, from 1814-1892.* (Cincinnati, Ohio: Weier & Daiker, Prs., 1892).

24. For a German-American history of the Civil War, see: Wilhelm Kaufmann, *Germans in the American Civil War: With a Biographical Directory*. Translated by Steven Rowan and edited by Don Heinrich Tolzmann with Werner D. Mueller and Robert E. Ward. (Carlisle, Pa.: John Kallmann, 1999), and for the role Cincinnati played in particular, see: Burgheim, *Cincinnati*, pp. 166-85, and also: *Cincinnati und sein Deutschthum: Elne Geschichte der Entwicklung Cincinnatis und seines Deutschthums, mit biographischen SKizzen und Illustrationen.* (Cincinnati, Ohio: Queen City Publishing Co., 1901), pp. 17-20.

25. The term "Lain farmer" refers to the well educated German immigrants, who came to the U.S. after the revolutions of the 1830s, and read Latin texts as they plowed the fields.

26. Regarding this historical journal, see: Mary Edmund Spanheimer, *The German Pioneer Legacy: The Life and Work of Heinrich A. Rattermann.* 2nd ed. Edited by Don Heinrich Tolzmann. (New York: Peter Lang Pub. Co., 2004), pp. 110-25.

27. For information on Rümelin's works, see: Robert E. Ward, *A Bio-Bibliography of German-American Writers, 1670-1970.* (White Plains, New York: Kraus International Publications, 1985), p. 251.

28. For biographical information about Klauprecht, see: Klauprecht, *German Chronicle*, pp. ix-xiv; Burgheim, *Cincinnati*, p. 123; and: Howe, *Hamilton County*, p. 116.

29. For a discussion of Klauprecht's history, see: Don Heinrich Tolzmann, *German-American Studies: Selected Essays*. (New York: Peter Lang Pub. Co., 2001), p. 11.

30. For biographical information about Martels, see: Ward, *A Bio-Bibliography*, pp. 189-90.

31. See: *Der Deutsche* Pioner. 10(1878): 317. Also, regarding Pulte, see: Koerner, *Das Deutsche Element*, p. 194, and: Howe, *Hamilton County*, p. 116.

32. For a biography of Rattermann, see: Burgheim, Cincinnati, pp. 549-53; Armin Tenner, *Cincinnati Sonst und Jetzt: Eine Geshichte Cincinnatis und seiner verdienstvollen Bürger deutscher Zunge mit biographischen Skizzen und Portraitillustrationen*. (Cincinnati: Mecklenborg & Rosenthal, 1878), pp. 397-402; and: Spanheimer, *The German Pioneer Legacy*, especially pp. 1-59.

33. See Rattermann's collected works: *Gesammelte ausgewählte Werke*. (Cincinnati, Ohio: Im Selbstverlage, 1906-12), 12 vols.

34. Regarding Rattermann's editorship of the journal, see: Spanheimer, *The German Pioneer Legacy*, pp. 110-25.

35. For information on the German Literary Club, see: Spanheimer, *The German Pioneer Legacy*, pp. 28-34, and: Burgheim, *Cincinnati*, p. 322-23.

36. Regarding Rattermann's library, see: Spanheimer, *The German Pioneer Legacy*, pp. 135-40

37. For the history of Rattermann's company, see: H. William Brockmann and H.A. Rattermann, *The Story of Our First Century of Service: A Memorial of the Hundredth Anniversary... May 10, 1958*. (Cincinnati, Ohio: Hamilton Mutual Insurance, 1958). This is an English update of Rattermann's 1908 history of the company.

Chapter 2

1. For further information about the Emigrant School, see: Klauprecht, *German Chronicle*, p. 175, and: Burgheim, *Cincinnati*, p. 81.

2. For the history of German instruction in Cincinnati, see: Carolyn R. Toth, *German-English Bilingual Schools in America: The Cincinnati Tradition in Historical Context.* (New York: Peter Lang Pub. Co., 1990).

3. Regarding Mühl, see: Klauprecht, *German Chronicle*, p. 177; Rattermann, *Werke*, Vol. 12, pp. 351-60; A.D. Falbisaner, *Eduard Mühl: Ein deutschamerikanischer Kämpfer für Freiheit und Menschenrechte.* (Philadelphia: German-American Annals Press, 1903 (also published in: *Americana Germanica.* 5:8(1903): 449-90; 5:9(1903): 519-54); H.A. Rattermann, "Einige Berichtigungen, *Americana Germanica.* 5:12(1903); 722-33, 752-55; John J. Weisert, "Eduard Mühl's Lichtfreund," *American German Review.* 22:4(1956): 30-31; and Don Heinrich Tolzmann, *Missouri's German Heritage.* 2nd ed. (Milford, Ohio: Little Miami Pub. Co., 2004), pp. 7, 12, 25, 36.

4. For further information about the movement for German instruction, see: Klauprecht, *German Chronicle*, pp. 175-76, and: Burgheim, *Cincinnati*, p. 81-85.

5. For biographical information on Rölker, see: H.A. Rattermann, *Werke*, Vol. 12, pp. 105-124.

6. Regarding von Löher's lecture series and publications, see: Don Heinrich Tolzmann, *German-American Studies: Selected Essays.* (New York: Peter Lang Pub. Co., 2001), p. 11. Also, see: Burgheim, *Cincinnati*, p. 144.

7. For information about Renz, see: Klauprecht, *German Chroncile*, p. 176-77; Rattermann, *Werke*, Vol. 12, pp. 105-24; and also: H.A. Rattermann, "Ein Vorkämpfer für das deutsche Schulsystem in den öffentlichen Schulen Cincinnatis," *Der Deutsche Pionier.* 6(1874): 75-81.

8. Regarding Hemann, see: Klauprecht, *German Chroncile*, p. 175; Rattemann, *Werke*, Vol. 12, pp. 105-24.

9. For information about Gerstäcker's stay in Cincinnati, see: Klauprecht, *German Chroncile*, p. 176; Rattermann, *Werke*, Vol. 12, pp. 67-79. Also, see: Burgheim, *Cincinnati*, p. 83.

10. For biographical information about Molitor, see: Klauprecht, *German Chronicle*, p. 176, and: Burgheim, *Cincinnati*, p. 125.

11. For biographical information on Rődter, see: Klauprecht, *German* Chronicle, p. 172; Rattermann, *Werke*, Vol. 12, pp. 225-96; "Heinrich Rődter," *Der Deutsche Pionier*. 1(1869): 130-33; and: Burghiem, *Cincinnati*, p. 130.

12. For Molitor's obituary, see: Karl Rűmelin, "Ein Nachruf an Stephan Molitor," *Der Deutsche Pionier*. 6(1874): 2-5.

13. Regarding Walker, see: Klauprecht, *German Chronicle*, pp. 173-74, 177; "Georg Walker," *Der Deutsche Pionier*. 4(1872): 141-49; and: Burgheim, *Cincinnati*, p. 120.

14. For information about Rehfuss, see: Klauprecht, *German Chronicle*, pp. 171-72, 185, and 189.

15. For information on Moor, see: Kaufmann, *Germans in the American Civil War*, p. 311-12.

16. For Tenner's biographical essay, see: Tenner, *Cincinnati*, pp. 36-40.

17. Regarding Kautz, see: Kaufmann, *Germans in the American Civil War*, pp. 274-75.

18. For information on Weitzel, see: Kaufmann, *Germans in the American Civil War*, p. 274.

19. See footnote no. 13 for information on Walker. Rattermann notes that the meeting was led by Molitor, editor of the *Volksblatt* (chairman of the meeting); Dr. C.F. Schmidt, publisher and editor of the *Republikaner* (secretary of the meeting), and Walker, editor of the *Volksbühne*).

20. Regarding biographical information about Krőll, see: Rattermann, *Werke*, Vol. 12, pp. 125-34.

21. See: H.A. Rattermann, "Nikolaus Hőffer," *Der Deutsche Pionier*. 6(1874): 419-26, with the page reference here being to p. 419.

Chapter 3

1. For biographical information on Krőll, see footnote 20, Chapter 1. Also, see: Max Burgheim, *Cincinnati in Wort und Bild. Mit zahlreichen Illustrationen.* (Cincinnati, Ohio: Burgheim Publishing Co., 1891), pp. 264, and: Tenner, *Cincinnati*, pp. 19-20.

2. For further information regarding German immigration and settlement in Missouri, see: Tolzmann, ed., *Missouri's German Heritage*, pp. 7-37.

3. For information about this church, see; Tolzmann, *German Heritage Guide to the Greater Cincinnati Area*, pp. 7, 79, 84.

4. Regarding this newspaper, see: Tolzmann, *Cincinnati's German Heritage*, Part I, pp. 54-55.

5. For information on Eckstein, see: Tolzmann, *Cincinnati's German Heritage*, Part I, pp. 92-93, and: Howe, *Hamilton County*, p. 123.

6. This unpublished lecture can be found in manuscript form in the Rattermann Collection at the University of Illinois-Urbana; a photocopy is also in the possession of the editor.

7. For the historical origins of German music in Cincinnati, see: Burgheim, *Cincinnati*, p.p. 88-114, 340-43, and: Tolzmann, *Cincinnati's German Heritage*, Part I, pp. 93-95.

8. Regarding Pike, see: Burgheim, *Cincinnati*, p. 335, and: Howe, *Hamilton County*, p. 117.

9. Jenny Lind was a Swedish opera singer, who toured the U.S., beginning in 1850.

10. James Fish was a New York financier, who was well known as "Big Jim" and Diamond Jim."

11. For further information about these participants in the uprisings of the 1830s, see: Koerner, *Das deutsche Element*, especially Chapter 3.

12. Regarding the founding of the first Turnverein in America, see: Burgheim, *Cincinnati*, pp. 153-58, 310-12, and: Tolzmann, *Cincinnati's German Heritage*, Part I, pp. 75-76.

13. For an introduction to the 1848 Revolution, see: Burgheim, Cincinnati, pp. 146-52, and: Don Heinrich Tolzmann, ed., *The German-American Forty-Eighters*,

1848-1998. (Indianapolis, Indiana: Indiana University-Purdue University, Max Kade German-American Center & Indiana German Heritage Society, 1997).

14. Regarding Stallo, see: Klauprecht, *German Chronicle*, pp. 182, 185, and 195-96; Burgheim, *Cincinnati*, p. 589; Howe, *Hamilton County*, p. 117; and: Rattermann, *Werke*, Vol. 12, pp. 9-54.

15. For bio-bibliographical information on Follen and Lieber, see: Ward, *A Bio-Bibliography*, pp. 83-84, 176-77.

16. Regarding Franz Joseph Stallo, see: Rattermann, *Werke*, Vol. 12, pp. 9-54.

17. For further information about Stallostown, which was later re-named Minster, see: *Souvenir of the One Hundredth Anniversary of the Founding of Minster, Ohio: Septmber 28, 1832-Sepember 28, 1932.* (Minster, Ohio: Post Printing Co., 1932).

18. For references to other works by Stallo, see: Ward, *A Bio-Bibliography*, p. 288.

19. Regarding Judge Bellamy Storer, see: Howe, *Hamilton County*, p. 60.

20. Koerner indicates that it is impossible to convey the spirit of Stallo's remarks by means of excerpts, but then contradicts himself by trying to do so by including an excerpt from Stallo's address. Although his remarks help us understand the case, their length interrupts the general flow of his history, causing the editor to place them here in the notes. Koerner cites Stallo's remarks as follows:

> I dispute the assertion not only that Christianity is the law of the land and that our democratic institutions rest on Christian civilization, but also that our civilization today in any sense of the word can be called a Christian one. With civilization we refer to the entire strengths and effects of the physical, intellectual and moral culture of a people. However, the magnificent accomplishments that shape our culture, as well as the advantages accruing to them, were won not by means of, but in spite of Christianity. It is not Christianity that has opened the intellectual horizon that for us is like an infinity of space; it is not Christianity that has revealed laws to us, according to which the stars and their satellites are formed and develop in the expanse of the universe and the obediently turn in their annual course under the invisible direction of unchanging attraction; it is not Christianity, which has revealed the mysteries of the

planetary system, or has given us the power to coordinate the elements to our willpower. Copernicus devoted his eternal work to the pope, but the pope sealed it from the eyes of believers, and his Inquisition locked up Galileo so he could not observe the heavens, because he dared to view it through a telescope and to recognize the truths regarding the centricity of the sun. However, not only the pope and the Catholic Church sought to extinguish the morning sun of a new era, or to block the view of awakening humankind. No, Luther and Melanchthon also condemned the Copernican system as strongly as Rome. When after the first centuries of the Apostolic Age did Christianity baptize one of the new truths that were born in order to relieve the world of a part of its burden or to alleviate its woes? Whenever now, or years ago, a faint glimmer of an unusual light appeared on the horizon, then the best way to find it was to look where the papacy and its Church committed their latest anathema, and where the Protestants cast their final curses. At this moment, all of Europe resounds again from the sound of the Church's artillery that is being fired at those, who attempt to ascribe the development of organic beings to the unchangeable laws of nature that govern the generation of all things in the universe.

Koerner then continues as follows:

> At this point, one of the judges, Storer, interrupted the speaker, asking: "Are you referring to the man, who is of the opinion that our ancestors are derived from the animal kingdom?"
>
> Stallo responded: "I definitely refer to Charles Darwin, who, not convincingly enough, has presented the theory that man has reached the highest step of organic development not by means of a miracle, but rather in one way or another, made it up the ladder step by step."

Chapter 4

1. For further information on the topics discussed relating to Columbus, see: LaVern J. Rippley, *The Columbus Germans*. (Indianapolis, Indiana: Max Kade German-

American Center, Indiana University-Purdue University at Indianapolis & Indiana German Heritage Society, 1998).

2. Information about the German-American newspapers in Columbus mentioned here and later can be found in: Rippley, *The Columbus Germans*, pp. 5-9.

3. For further information about Friedrich Fieser, see: Friedrich Fieser, "Aus meinen Erinnerungen," *Der Deutsche Pionier*. 1(1869): 273-77.

4. Regarding German churches in Columbus, see: Rippley, *The Columbus Germans*, pp. 30-36.

5. For further information about Peter Kaufmann, see: Karl J.R. Arndt, ed., *Teutonic Visions of Social Perfection for Emerson/Verheissung und Erfüllung: A Documentary History of Peter Kaufmann's Quest for Social Perfection from Geroge Rapp to Ralph Waldo Emerson.* (Worcester, Massachusetts: The Harmony Press, 1998).

6. For the history of the Cleveland Germans, see: Steven Rowan, ed., *Cleveland and its Germans.* (Cleveland, Ohio: Western Reserve Historical Society, 1998), 2 vols., and also by the same editor: *Jubilee Edition of the Cleveland Wächter und Anzeiger, 1902.* (Cleveland, Ohio: Western Reserve Historical Society, 2000).

7. For a biographical article about Bösel, see: "Karl Bösel," *Der Deutsche Pionier*. 17(1885): 210-25. Also, see the following articles: Karl Bösel, "Ansiedlung von New-Bremen," *Der Deutsche Pionier*. 1(1869): 84-87, 118-21, and also by him: "Einwanderers Abenteuer," *Der Deutsche Pionier*. 3(1871)> 215-17.

Chapter 5

1. This is a translation of Koerner's chapter on Kentucky, part of which appeared in: H.A. Rattermann, *Kentucky's German Pioneers: H.A. Rattermann's History.* Translated and edited by Don Heinrich Tolzmann. (Bowie, Maryland: Heritage Books, Inc., 2001), pp. 95-101.

2. For a history and directory of German-American businesses in Louisville, see: *Louisville Anzeiger: Jubiläums-Beilage. Zum Eintritt in das 61te Jahr seines Bestehens, 1849-1909.* (Louisville, Kentucky: Tinsley-Mayer Engraving Co., 1909; reprinted: Louisville: Louisville Breweries Book, 1998).

3. See: Kaufmann, *Germans in the American Civil War*, p. 277.

4. For further information about the German-American response to the unification of Germany, see: Tolzmann, *German-American Experience*, pp. 219ff.

5. Regarding nativism, see: Ibid, pp. 199 ff.

6. Note that the German-American press up and down the Ohio River and throughout the entire river valley was closely interrelated, with editors and publishers often moving from town to town, especially back and forth between Louisville and Cincinnati.

7. For biographical information on Klauprecht, see Chapter One, footnote no. 28.

8. For a discussion of nativism in Philadelphia, see: Koerner, *Das Deutsche Element*, especially the first three chapters dealing with Pennsylvania.

9. For further information on nativism in Louisville, see: Elsie Rowell, "The Social and Cultural Contributions of the Germans in Louisville from 1848-1855," M.A. Thesis, University of Kentucky, 1941.

10. Koerner here makes to reference to: Ludwig Stierlin, *Der Staat Kentucky und die Stadt Louisville, mit besonderer Berücksichtigung des deutschen Elements.* (Louisville, 1873).

11. Here Koerner notes that his primary focus is in the period up to 1848, although he has already covered items thereafter relating to the Civil War.

12. Regarding the Forty-Eighters, see: Tolzmann, ed., *The German-American Forty-Eighters, 1848-1998.*

13. Regarding the cities Koerner's mentions here, see: Rattermann, *Kentucky's German Pioneers*, pp. 1-65.

14. Ibid.

Chapter 6 - Indiana

1. For the history of the German element of Indianapolis, see: George Theodore Probst, *The Germans in Indianapolis, 1840-1918.* Revised and illustrated edition by Eberhard Reichmann. (Indianapolis: German-American Center & Indiana German Heritage Society, 1989).

2. For the section of Koerner's history relating to Rapp, see: Koerner, *The German Element in the Northeast*, pp. 14-16.

3. See: Karl J.R. Arndt, *George Rapp's Harmony Society, 1785-1847.* (Rutherford: Fairleigh Dickinson University Press, 1871).

4. For the Duke's report, see: Bernhard, Duke of Saxe-Weimar-Eisenach, *Travels of His Highness duke Bernhard of Saxe-Weimar-Eisenach through North America in the Years 1825 and 1826.* Translated by William Jeronimus and edited by C.J. Jeronimus. (Lanham, Maryland: University Press of America, 2001).

5. For a history of the settlement along the Ohio River, see: Karl J.R. Arndt, ed., *George Rapp's Years of Glory: Economy on the Ohio.* (New York: Peter Lang Pub. Co., 1987).

6. See: Karl J.R. Arndt, *A Documentary History of the Indiana Decade of the Harmony Society, 1814-1824.* 2 vols. (Indianapolis: Indiana Historical Society, 1975).

7. For further information regarding the travel reports that Koerner mentions here, see: Reuben Gold Thwaites, ed., *Early Western Travels, 1748-1846: A Series of Annotated Reprints of Some of the Best and Rarest Contemporary Volumes of Travel, Decription of the Aborigines and Social and Economic Conditions in the Middle and Far West, During the Period of the Early American Settlement.* 32 vols. (Cleveland, Ohio: A.H. Clark, 1904-07).

8. Regarding Astor (1763-1848), and his family, see: Lucy Kavaler, *The Astors: AN American Legend.* (New York: Dodd, Mead, 1968), and also by the same author: *The Astors: A Family Chronicle of Pomp and Circumstance.* (New York: Dodd, Mead, 1966).

Chapter 7

1. See: Alexander Schem, ed., *Deutsch-Amerikanisches Conversations-Lexikon.* (New York: Ernst Steiger, 1869-73).

2. See: Shirley J. Riemer, *The German Research Companion.* New revised edition. (Sacramento, California: Lorelei Press, 2000), pp. 221-24..

3. For coverage of this recent time period of German-American history, see: Tolzmann, *The German-American Experience*, pp. 349ff.

About the Editor

Don Heinrich Tolzmann is the author and editor of numerous books on German-American history and culture; he has received many awards, including the Federal Cross of Merit from Germany, the Ohioana Book Award, the German-American of the Year Award, and the Outstanding Achievement Award of the Society for German-American Studies. Retired as Curator of the German-Americana Collection and Director of German-American Studies at the University of Cincinnati, Tolzmann serves as President of the German-American Citizens League of Greater Cincinnati, as well as Curator of the League's German Heritage Museum.

Index

CPSIA information can be obtained at www.ICGtesting.com
Printed in the USA
LVOW060924310513

336042LV00012B/427/P